The ~~[Cut]~~ Shakespeare

The plays of Shakespeare edited by Steve Gooch

with a Foreword by Oliver Ford Davies

COMED

GW00703287

Twelfth
Much Ado abo

Steve Gooch Publications

First published in Great Britain in 2006 by
Steve Gooch Publications
PO BOX 5, Robertsbridge, East Sussex, TN32 5ZS

ISBN: 0-9553282-0-9
ISBN 13: 978-0-9553282-0-6

Printed and Bound by Antony Rowe Ltd
Chippenham, Wiltshire SN14 6LH

Contents

Acknowledgements

The process of editing these texts has taken me through a succession of discoveries about the pros and cons of presenting Shakespeare, not only in his words but also in modern typography, spelling, punctuation and so on. Throughout this process I have consulted with school teachers, drama schools and theatre practitioners of my acquaintance, whose advice and feedback has been invaluable. I should particularly like to mention the constant advice and practical help I've received from Pauline Courtice, Peggy Paterson, Jane Noble, Meg Beckett, Chris Barlas and Nikki Atkin-Reeves, as well as excellent feedback from productions in performance by John Abbott, Terrie Fender, Christine Kimberley and Michael Punter.

S.G.

Foreword

Having spent twelve years at the Royal Shakespeare Company, and acted in twenty-four of the plays, I know that the cutting of the text is a complicated but crucial art. Some doom-mongers suggest that with the declining interest in language throughout society the plays will be thought too archaic for production by 2050. But I find that Shakespeare's language communicates at a deeper level than the literal meaning of the words. His imagery – 'Pity, like a new-born babe striding the blast' – can go straight to the gut, by-passing the rational mind. At the same time Shakespeare is not always accessible. He sometimes over-writes, uses six images where two would be more telling, dives into byways which, however diverting, slacken the interest of the story, and invents language which is intractably difficult.

We know from the quarto and folio *King Lear* that Shakespeare almost certainly cut his own plays. The quarto *Henry V*, which cuts the 3400 lines to 1700, suggests that much streamlining went on to achieve 'the two hours' traffic of our stage'. Shakespeare may never have seen *Hamlet* in its entirety – and if he had, might have taken the blue pencil to it immediately. *The Cut Shakespeare* goes back therefore to the Globe, and Steve Gooch is in an honourable tradition. He has trimmed the plays with great ingenuity and discretion, and has taken the helpful decision to print the complete text. School, amateur and many professional directors will benefit enormously from his suggestions. As he writes, 'It is playability and story-telling which have won out'. With such sympathetic cutting Shakespeare should be alive and well in 2050 ... and 2150.

Oliver Ford Davies

INTRODUCTION

These editions are meant to be spoken aloud rather than as private reading matter. Whether in full production or simply read in class, the aim is to bring professional, script-editing skills to the aid of directors and teachers at all levels, but without prejudicing their final choices. The thinking behind 'The Cut Shakespeare' originated partly from witnessing actors struggle with Shakespeare's language in productions by schools and amateurs – and indeed some professionals – but partly also from my experience of editing scripts as a literary manager and teacher of playwriting. Whereas the reading problem can be addressed by bringing actors to understand what's going on *behind* the lines, making the author's own intentions clearer and more vivid is often best achieved by removing material which gets in the way – 'seeing the wood for the trees'.

In recent years Shakespeare's reputation for accessibility has dipped sharply. Whatever the reasons for this change in public perception, there is a danger that a cornerstone of our national culture is dismissed out of hand for lack of direct knowledge. As an amateur production of *A Midsummer Night's Dream* in my own village revealed, people can be frightened off Shakespeare if they're thinking more about the words than the deeds. Rather than modernise or adapt the originals and risk giving a false impression of them, why not let them speak more keenly for themselves?

In order for any text to be performed well it has first to be understood and 'internalised', that is, an actor has to connect to the life behind the words. In the case of Shakespeare this would mean connecting to the life of four centuries ago. Too often in performances of Shakespeare, actors (both amateur and professional) settle for delivering 'difficult' lines in a superficial, generalised style, mimicked acoustically from previously witnessed productions, without making them truly their own. By having potential cuts indicated in advance, directors and actors may save energy often spent wrestling with the text in preparation and -- more acutely -- rehearsal, and find a delivery more vivid to modern consciousness. At the same time they would be encouraged to focus on the qualities of characterisation and storytelling which are the joys of Shakespeare in performance.

The text could have been presented purely in cut form. Editing a play can be an extremely time-consuming and brain-twisting exercise. But to withhold large sections of text without comeback seemed to me to prejudice people's judgement too far. It is one thing to be assisted in what can be a complicated task; it is another to have your mind made up for you. Therefore the text to be acted has been presented in as bold and readable a form as possible, while potential cuts are indicated in a fainter, thinner typeface. In this way the excised sections are still present in the background, can still be referred to in order to enhance the reader's overall understanding of the played text, and can be restored for performance if desired. When presented with the choice between Quarto and Folio I have tended to opt for the latter, except where the former is more readily understood. With the more problematic texts like *Richard III*, to take account of recent scholarship I've sometimes even added all the passages that can be sensibly made to hang together and then 'cut' them.

As far as punctuation goes, I have tried to be consistent. But Shakespeare's syntax changes over the decades of his writing, so the flow can often *feel* different from play to play. To that extent I have taken each case on its own merits, being guided by meaning more than dogma. Beyond that I have tried to simplify and modernise, opting for an approach which I feel will aid a first-time reader aloud to stumble least on the lines while not being 'led' in their delivery. Not the least consideration in this respect is what will aid breathing and timing. For this reason I have followed the custom of contemporary playtexts and ignored 'traditional' grammar: sentences start with 'and' and 'but', and semicolons only appear where they seem more appropriate than the less daunting alternatives. I've made occasional use of '...' where a speech (rarely) seems to tail off or (more often) ends on a hesitant or expectant note; in the middle of a speech it can be useful to suggest a character's broken train of thought. I've also made regular use of the dash, sometimes to indicate where characters interrupt each other, sometimes where a character changes the person they're speaking to, and occasionally to indicate a change of tack. The dash has also been useful as a link where there is no other satisfactory way to provide a single punctuation that works for both the cut and the uncut versions.

Where iambic rhythm demands that past participles are intended to be accented – *veilèd, renownèd* – I have inserted accents, except at the ends of lines, where I prefer to leave it to the judgement (and ear) of the reader. The latter becomes crucial over something like the play on the word 'banished' in *Romeo and Juliet*. Conversely, where an actor might be tempted to stress a participle that would ruin the metre, I've apostrophised it – but removed apostrophes wherever they make a word look strange on the page, although, for example 'woman'd' is probably easier on a first sight-reading than 'womaned'. On a similar tack, there are some very rare occasions where phrases like 'I would' and 'I will' reduce to 'I'd' or 'I'll' without spoiling (and sometimes even enhancing) the metre.

The tendency in recent decades has been to remove exclamation marks where not obviously needed. My general principle has been to use every available form of punctuation to nuance speech if it makes the continuity of text clearer. And so I've felt it reasonable to re-insert exclamation marks to indicate what I can only describe as a 'non-conversational' tone, something more emphatic than ordinary discourse. Also, with quotation marks I've widened the punctuation vocabulary to use double quotes where a character is reporting (and possibly even mimicking) someone else's speech, as this flags up the difference more strongly to the sight-reader. Foreign words are differentiated by being in both bold and italics.

With spelling I've once again tried to opt for the form most recognisable to the contemporary eye. Recent scholarship has been particularly good at restoring some spellings to a more familiar form, an example I have followed except where play on the original word (even just its sound) may enrich the physical speaking of a scene. A similar desire to make everything self-explanatory lies behind removing roman numerals in act and scene numbering and having a List of Characters rather than *Dramatis Personae.*

Stage directions have in general been brought more into line with contemporary conventions, the most important thing being that the reader always knows *what is happening physically* on stage. In order not to over-prejudice the settings of scenes, I have included but bracketed the, often helpful, editorial assumptions of earlier editions.

Shakespeare can be wordy. There is some evidence that this was commented on in his own time, but in any case to remain immediately accessible for four centuries would be a tall order for language which is primarily meant to be spoken. There are even passages where I sense the author may have been called on to drag the proceedings out for a scene or costume change. Generally however, the principles behind my editing have been technical rather than ideological. Inevitably matters of personal taste have arisen. There are a few cases of glaringly obscure words or phrases which – once you've worked them out – are so pertinent or original ('mouth-honour' in *Macbeth* is a case in point) that I simply couldn't bear to cut them. And sometimes one can imagine an actor making them instantly clear simply by a telling delivery. But in the main I have tried to stick to the more 'objective' criteria of what is necessary to tell the story and reveal the characters. For example, in conducting research into the need for this series, one teacher reminded me that plays are often read in schools in a double period, but rarely completed. So the simple matter of overall playing time is one consideration. But *Hamlet* and *Richard III* are not the same length as *A Midsummer Night's Dream* or *Twelfth Night*, and nowhere have I attempted to reduce the plays to the same result. It's more important that the distinctiveness of the originals remain than that a reductive concept – whether technical, moral or social – is laid upon them.

In consequence I've resisted excising whole sections or scenes which are sometimes omitted in production – Jacques' 'Melancholy Song' in *As You Like It* for example – because that's easy enough for producers to do of their own accord. Rather, I have preferred in these sections to make heavy cuts of a kind which might not occur to the inexperienced, and leave the decision of wholesale cutting to the individual producer. Similarly there are places where I could have cut repetition or archaism more extensively than just a line or two, but considerations of metre or characterisation have made me pull back, knowing that once attention has been drawn to a particular passage, others may choose for themselves.

The progress of the plays also depends to a certain extent on the theatrical conventions of the day. Verbal exposition of background plot, for example, is a common feature and not the turn-off it is for today's audiences reared on film and television. Vague and often undeveloped reasons for getting characters on and off stage may also seem unnecessary to modern sensibilities. And I have regularly targeted the Shakespearian reflex for long, parenthetical similes, which are a mouthful for fully-trained professionals let alone an amateur or a child in school.

Sometimes the criterion is simply, 'Is it necessary?' An example is the end of Touchstone's speech in Act Three, Scene 3 of *As You Like It*, introducing the entrance of Sir Oliver Martext. A director might feel the need to have him say "Here comes Sir Oliver", but not only is this followed by his entrance but "Sir Oliver, you are well met". By then one might hope the audience has twigged who he is.

Shakespeare the poet is responsible for some of the most beautiful lines in dramatic literature, but he is also responsible for some excruciating puns, dreadful jokes, over-elaborate conceits and impenetrable rhetoric. Whereas the former, I hope, have always been kept in (even when they hold up the action), the latter have been regularly targeted for editing. In addition, there are occasional passages, perhaps quite beautiful in themselves but in which the language is so archaic that it has lost most of its meaning to a modern reader – and certainly to a first-time listener. Repetition and other rhetorical flourishes more familiar in Elizabethan theatre, I've also targeted where they do not contribute to plot or characterisation.

Inevitably there are passages where an intimate 'knowledge of the footnotes' would reveal those striking insights into the human condition which make Shakespeare unique; but one knows these will never be picked up on a single reading or hearing. Against that, the gesture behind individual lines in any dramatic dialogue can often become clearer when heard aloud in context. Indeed the dynamic of the situation can often make meaningful what would otherwise be a fog of words. So also with nonsense which is *playable* nonsense. 'I did impeticos thy gratility' The Clown says in *Twelfth Night*, which may not only be fun in the saying or playing, but without phrases like it one would lose totally the flavour of Elizabethan humour.

Rhythm can be important. Very occasionally I've taken tiny 'pleats' out in the middle of speeches – even cutting into the middle of lines – so that a scene can proceed according to our modern sensibility of dramatic pace rather than the statelier progress of the Elizabethan stage. Where possible, I've tried to tie these back in so the pentameter remains intact, or the line at least sounds complete. By the same token I've sometimes made tiny cuts in the middle of prose speeches where there are archaisms or where I feel the pudding is over-egged. More of these 'nips and tucks' might have been possible, but I've also borne in mind that these texts will often be sight-read, so I've tried to keep the changes of typeface easy on the eye, in order to be easy on the ear. Occasionally, where there are two passages of verse illustrating the same point differently, I have chosen to cut that which fits the metre rather than that which is more archaic, since the rhythm of the overall speech would otherwise be obtrusively disrupted.

Finally there are also those familiar passages – particularly at the end of scenes in the early plays – where the verse forms are more intricate than Shakespeare's customary blank verse, sometimes rhyming to lend finality to a character's last words. In these places, if you're not to destroy the rhythm – or more disastrously the rhyme – you have to cut all or nothing. Where I've left the whole thing, it's because I've felt the scene would seem incomplete with nothing at all. Within these considerations I've been as strict as possible about maintaining the original iambic pentameter, especially in those plays where its use is regular – even those tricky moments where lines are split between characters. Similarly, in prose sections, I've sometimes left in an impenetrable archaism where I feel it would otherwise rob an actor, and indeed the audience, of some necessary aspect of character.

But Shakespeare's unfamiliar language is not finally the principal consideration. Above all, it is essential to tell the story clearly. Quite often it becomes clearer for having extraneous matter removed. The faults of age in the text have finally to be balanced against the needs of the plot. Sometimes it is important to indicate in a difficult speech aspects of character whose importance will emerge only slowly; or touch in 'trails' of plot on which the action will turn crucially later on. Sometimes a touch of 'back story' will be sketched in with such imagination that you're almost living the character's life with it. These moments (though maybe not essential in Hollywood terms) I've kept in, as I have the odd line where cutting the one next to it makes it stand out better.

On the other hand I've had absolutely no consideration for equalising actors' parts. This seems to me a matter for the politics of production, more than the health of the play. I have even suggested the removal of complete roles where I feel they are so marginal to the action as to be an extravagance for the often pinched circumstances of contemporary production – or maybe offer an unsatisfying part for an actor.

If in doubt I've used the acid test of whether there is 'something to play', a clear action, response or intention behind the line as opposed to just words. In general then it is 'playability' and story-telling which have won out over more scholarly or literary considerations. Apart from those lines which are essential to the story – or too famous or beautifully turned ever to be cut by anyone – I have generally tried to pare the plays back to the shortest possible version the story will allow, in the secure knowledge that producers can put their own favourite bits back in. The resulting scripts cannot please everyone, but I hope they will reach out to more than would otherwise be the case.

Steve Gooch

Twelfth Night

or 'What You Will'

by William Shakespeare

LIST OF CHARACTERS

ORSINO	Duke of Illyria
SEBASTIAN	brother of Viola
ANTONIO	sea-captain, friend to Sebastian
A SEA CAPTAIN	to Viola
VALENTINE	gentleman attending on the Duke
[CURIO]	"
SIR TOBY BELCH	uncle to Olivia
SIR ANDREW AGUECHEEK	
MALVOLIO	steward to Olivia
FABIAN	servant to Olivia
FESTE	a clown, jester to Olivia
OLIVIA	a Countess
VIOLA	sister of Sebastian
MARIA	Olivia's woman ('GENTLEWOMAN')

1st OFFICER
2nd OFFICER
SERVANT
[LORDS, A PRIEST, SAILORS, MUSICIANS & ATTENDANTS]

Scene: *Illyria*

ACT ONE

Scene 1   *[Duke's Orsino's palace.]*
Enter DUKE ORSINO, [CURIO, other LORDS and MUSICIANS].

ORSINO   **If music be the food of love, play on,**
Give me excess of it that – surfeiting –
The appetite may sicken, and so die.
– That strain again. It had a dying fall.
O, it came o'er my ear like the sweet sound
10   **That breathes upon a bank of violets,**
Stealing and giving odour. – Enough, no more!
'Tis not so sweet now as it was before.
[O spirit of love, how quick and fresh art thou,
That, notwithstanding thy capacity
Receiveth as the sea, nought enters there,
Of what validity and pitch soe'er,
But falls into abatement and low price,
Even in a minute. So full of shapes is fancy
That it alone is high fantastical.
20

CURIO   Will you go hunt, my lord?

ORSINO   What, Curio?

CURIO   The hart.]

ORSINO   [Why, so I do, the noblest that I have.]
O, when mine eyes did see Olivia first,
Methought she purged the air of pestilence.
30   [That instant was I turned into a hart;
And my desires, like fell and cruel hounds,
E'er since pursue me.]
   (Enter VALENTINE)
How now, what news from her?

VALENTINE So please my lord, I might not be admitted,
But from her handmaid do return this answer:
[The element itself, till seven years' heat,
Shall not behold her face at ample view;
40   But,] **like a cloistress, she will veilèd walk**
And water once a day her chamber round
With eye-offending brine. All this to season
A brother's dead love, which she would keep fresh
And lasting in her sad remembrance.

ORSINO   **O, she that hath a heart of that fine frame**
To pay this debt of love but to a brother,
How will she love[, when the rich golden shaft
Hath killed the flock of all affections else
50   That live in her;] **when liver, brain and heart,**
These sovereign thrones, are all supplied – and filled
Her sweet perfections with one self king!
Away before me to sweet beds of flowers.
Love-thoughts lie rich when canopied with bowers.   *(Exeunt)*

Scene 2 *[The sea-coast.]*
Enter VIOLA, a CAPTAIN [and SAILORS].

VIOLA **What country, friends, is this?**

CAPTAIN **This is Illyria, lady.**

VIOLA **And what should I do in Illyria?**
My brother he is in Elysium.

10 **Perchance he is not drowned. — What think you**[, sailors]**?**

CAPTAIN **It is perchance that you yourself were saved.**

VIOLA **O my poor brother, and so perchance may he be.**

CAPTAIN **True, madam. And, to comfort you with chance,**
Assure yourself, after our ship did split,
When you and those poor number saved with you
Hung on our driving boat, I saw your brother,

20 **Most provident in peril, bind himself**
[-- Courage and hope both teaching him the practise --]
To a strong mast that lived upon the sea —
[Where, like Arion on the dolphin's back,
I saw him hold acquaintance with the waves
So long as I could see.]

VIOLA **For saying so, there's gold.**
[Mine own escape unfoldeth to my hope,
Whereto thy speech serves for authority,

30 The like of him.] **Know'st thou this country?**

CAPTAIN **Ay, madam, well, for I was bred and born**
Not three hours' travel from this very place.

VIOLA **Who governs here?**

CAPTAIN **A noble duke, in nature**
As in name.

40 **VIOLA** **What is the name?**

CAPTAIN **Orsino.**

VIOLA **Orsino ... I have heard my father name him.**
He was a bachelor then.

CAPTAIN **And so is now, or was so very late.**
For but a month ago I went from hence,
And then 'twas fresh in murmur (as, you know,

50 **What great ones do the less will prattle of)**
That he did seek the love of fair Olivia.

VIOLA **What's she?**

CAPTAIN **A virtuous maid, the daughter of a count**
That died some twelvemonth since, then leaving her
In the protection of his son, her brother,
Who shortly also died; for whose dear love,
They say, she hath abjured the company

60 **And sight of men.**

VIOLA **O that I served that lady!**
[And might not be delivered to the world,
Till I had made mine own occasion mellow,
What my estate is!]

CAPTAIN **That were hard to compass,**
Because she will admit no kind of suit --
70 **No, not the Duke's.**

VIOLA **There is a fair behaviour in thee, captain;**
[And though that nature with a beauteous wall
Doth oft close in pollution, yet of thee
I will believe thou hast a mind that suits
With this thy fair and outward character.
I prithee – and I'll pay thee bounteously –
Conceal me what I am, and be my aid
For such disguise as haply shall become
The form of my intent. I'll serve this duke.
80 **Thou shall present me as an eunuch to him.**
It may be worth thy pains, for I can sing
And speak to him in many sorts of music
That will allow me very worth his service.
[What else may hap to time I will commit.
Only shape thou thy silence to my wit.]

CAPTAIN **Be you his eunuch, and your mute I'll be.**
When my tongue blabs, then let mine eyes not see.

90 **VIOLA** **I thank thee. Lead me on.** *(Exeunt)*

Scene 3 *[A room in Olivia's house.]*
Enter SIR TOBY BELCH and MARIA.

SIR TOBY **What a plague means my niece to take the death of**
her brother thus? I am sure care's an enemy to life.

MARIA **By my troth, Sir Toby, you must come in earlier o'**
nights. Your cousin, my lady, takes great exceptions to your ill
10 **hours.**

[SIR TOBY Why, let her except, before excepted.

MARIA Ay, but you must confine yourself within the modest limits of order.

SIR TOBY Confine! I'll confine myself no finer than I am. These clothes are good
enough to drink in; and so be these boots too. An they be not, let them hang themselves
in their own straps.]

MARIA [That quaffing and drinking will undo you.] **I heard my lady talk**
20 **of it yesterday, and of a foolish knight that you brought in one**
night here to be her wooer.

SIR TOBY **Who, Sir Andrew Aguecheek?**

MARIA **Ay, he.**

13

	SIR TOBY	He's as tall a man as any's in Illyria.
30	MARIA	What's that to the purpose?
	SIR TOBY	Why, he has three thousand ducats a year.

MARIA   Ay, but [he'll have but a year in all these ducats;] he's a very fool and a prodigal.

SIR TOBY   Fie, that you'll say so! He [plays o' the *viol-de-gamboys*, and] speaks three or four languages word for word without book, and hath all the good gifts of nature.

40   MARIA   He hath indeed, [almost natural;] for besides that he's a fool, he's a great quarreller; and but that he hath the gift of a coward [to allay the gust he hath in quarrelling], 'tis thought among the prudent he would quickly have the gift of a grave.

sodding [handwritten annotation in left margin]

SIR TOBY   By this hand, they are scoundrels and subtractors that say so of him. Who are they?

MARIA   They that add, moreover, he's drunk nightly in your company.

50

SIR TOBY   With drinking healths to my niece. I'll drink to her as long as there is a passage in my throat and drink in Illyria. He's a coward and a coystrel that will not drink to my niece till his brains turn -- [o' the toe like a parish-top. What, wench! *Castiliano vulgo*, for here comes Sir Andrew Agueface.]

    Enter SIR ANDREW.

	ANDREW	Sir Toby Belch! How now, Sir Toby Belch?
60	SIR TOBY	Sweet Sir Andrew!
	ANDREW	Bless you, fair shrew.
	MARIA	And you too, sir.
	SIR TOBY	Accost, Sir Andrew, accost.
70	ANDREW	What's that?
	SIR TOBY	My niece's chambermaid.
	ANDREW	Good Mistress Accost, I desire better acquaintance.
	MARIA	My name is Mary, sir.
	ANDREW	Good Mistress Mary Accost --

SIR TOBY   You mistake, knight. 'Accost' is front her, board her, woo her, assail her.

80

ANDREW   By my troth, I would not undertake her in this company. -- Is that the meaning of 'accost'?

MARIA   Fare you well, gentlemen.

SIR TOBY   An thou let part so, Sir Andrew, would thou mightst never draw sword again.

90 **ANDREW   An you part so, mistress, I would I might never draw sword again. Fair lady, do you think you have fools in hand?**

MARIA   Sir, I have not you by the hand.

[ANDREW   Marry, but you shall have -- and here's my hand.

MARIA   Now, sir, 'thought is free'. I pray you, bring your hand to the buttery-bar
and let it drink.

100 ANDREW   Wherefore, sweetheart? What's your metaphor?

MARIA   It's dry, sir.

ANDREW   Why, I think so. I am not such an ass but I can keep my hand dry. But
what's your jest?

MARIA   A dry jest, sir.

ANDREW   Are you full of them?
110

MARIA   Ay, sir, I have them at my fingers' ends. Marry, now I let go your hand,
I am barren.]   *(Exit)*

SIR TOBY   O knight, [thou lackest a cup of canary --] **when did I see thee so put down?**

ANDREW   [Never in your life, I think, unless you see canary put me down.]
**Methinks sometimes I have no more wit than a Christian or an
ordinary man has. But I am a great eater of beef and I believe that**
120 **does harm to my wit.**

SIR TOBY   No question.

**ANDREW   An I thought that, I'd forswear it. I'll ride home
tomorrow, Sir Toby.**

SIR TOBY   *Pourquoi*, my dear knight?

ANDREW   What is *'pourquoi'*? Do or not do? I would I had
130 **bestowed that time in the tongues that I have in fencing, dancing
and bear-baiting ... O, had I but followed the arts!**

SIR TOBY   Then hadst thou had an excellent head of hair.

ANDREW   Why, would that have mended my hair?

SIR TOBY   Past question; for thou seest it will not curl by nature.

ANDREW   But it becomes me well enough, does't not?
140

**SIR TOBY   Excellent. It hangs like flax on a distaff, and I hope to
see a housewife take thee between her legs and spin it off.**

**ANDREW   Faith, I'll home tomorrow, Sir Toby. Your niece will
not be seen. Or if she be, it's four to one she'll none of me. The
Count himself here hard by woos her.**

**SIR TOBY   She'll none o' the Count. She'll not match above her
degree, neither in estate, years, nor wit. I have heard her swear't.**
150 **Tut, there's life in't, man.**

15

ANDREW   I'll stay a month longer. I am a fellow o' the strangest mind i' the world ... I delight in masques and revels sometimes altogether.

SIR TOBY   Art thou good at these *kickshawses*, knight?

[ANDREW   As any man in Illyria, whatsoever he be, under the degree of my betters; and yet I will not compare with an old man.

160

SIR TOBY   What is thy excellence in a *galliard*, knight?]

ANDREW   Faith, I can cut a caper.

[SIR TOBY   And I can cut the mutton to't.]

ANDREW   And I think I have the back-trick simply as strong as any man in Illyria.

170   **SIR TOBY**   Wherefore are these things hid? [Wherefore have these gifts a curtain before 'em? Are they like to take dust, like Mistress Mall's picture? Why dost thou not go to church in a *galliard* and come home in a *coranto*? My very walk should be a jig. I would not so much as make water but in a *sink-a-pace*. What dost thou mean?] Is it a world to hide virtues in? I did think, by the excellent constitution of thy leg, it was formed under the star of a *galliard*.

ANDREW   Ay, 'tis strong, and it does indifferent well in a flame-coloured stock. Shall we set about some revels?

180   **SIR TOBY**   What shall we do else? Were we not born under Taurus?

ANDREW   Taurus ... that's sides and heart.

SIR TOBY   No, sir, it is legs and thighs. Let me see thee caper. Ha, higher! Ha, ha, excellent!   *(Exeunt)*

Scene 4   *[A room in the Duke's palace.]*
              Enter VALENTINE and VIOLA in man's attire.

VALENTINE If the Duke continue these favours towards you, Cesario, you are like to be much advanced. He hath known you but three days, and already you are no stranger.

VIOLA   [You either fear his humour or my negligence, that you call in question the continuance of his love.] Is he inconstant, sir, in his favours?

10

VALENTINE No, believe me.

VIOLA   I thank you. Here comes the Count.

              Enter DUKE ORSINO, [CURIO and Attendants].

ORSINO   Who saw Cesario, ho?

VIOLA   On your attendance, my lord, here.

20

ORSINO   *[(To Curio)]* Stand you a while aloof. – Cesario,
Thou know'st no less but all. I have unclasped
To thee the book e'en of my secret soul.

16

Therefore, good youth, address thy gait unto her,
Be not denied access, stand at her doors,
And tell them, there thy fixèd foot shall grow
Till thou have audience.

30 [VIOLA   Sure, my noble lord,
If she be so abandoned to her sorrow
As it is spoke, she never will admit me.

ORSINO   Be clamorous and leap all civil bounds
Rather than make unprofited return.]

VIOLA   Say I do speak with her, my lord, what then?

ORSINO   O, then unfold the passion of my love,
Surprise her with discourse of my dear faith.
40 **It shall become thee well to act my woes –**
[She will attend it better in thy youth
Than in a *nuncio*'s of more grave aspect.]

VIOLA   I think not so, my lord.

ORSINO   Dear lad, believe it –
For they shall yet belie thy happy years
That say thou art a man. Diana's lip
Is not more smooth and rubious; thy small pipe
50 **Is as the maiden's organ, shrill and sound;**
And all is semblative a woman's part.
[I know thy constellation is right apt
For this affair. Some four or five attend him --
All, if you will, for I myself am best
When least in company.] **Prosper well in this,**
And thou shalt live as freely as thy lord,
To call his fortunes thine.

VIOLA   I'll do my best
60 **To woo your lady.** *(Aside)* **Yet, a barful strife!**
Whoe'er I woo, myself would be his wife.   *(Exeunt)*

Scene 5   *[A room in Olivia's house.]*
                    Enter MARIA and FESTE.

MARIA   Nay, either tell me where thou hast been, or I will not
open my lips so wide as a bristle may enter in way of thy excuse.
My lady will hang thee for thy absence.

FESTE   Let her hang me. He that is well hanged in this world
needs to fear no colours.
10
MARIA   Make that good.

FESTE   He shall see none to fear.

[MARIA   A good lenten answer. I can tell thee where that saying was born, of 'I
fear no colours.'

FESTE   Where, good Mistress Mary?

17

MARIA   In the wars -- and that may you be bold to say in your foolery.

FESTE   Well, God give them wisdom that have it. And those that are fools, let them use their talents.]

MARIA   **Yet you will be hanged for being so long absent.** [Or, to be turned away, is not that as good as a hanging to you?

FESTE   Many a good hanging prevents a bad marriage. And, for turning away, let summer bear it out.

30

MARIA   You are resolute, then?]

FESTE   **Not so, neither, but I am resolved on two points.**

MARIA   **That if one break, the other will hold; or, if both break, your gaskins fall.**

FESTE   **Apt, in good faith, very apt.** [Well, go thy way, if Sir Toby would leave drinking, thou wert as witty a piece of Eve's flesh as any in Illyria.]

40

MARIA   [Peace, you rogue, no more o' that.] **Here comes my lady. Make your excuse wisely, you were best.**   *(Exit)*

FESTE   **Wit, an't be thy will, put me into good fooling.** [Those wits that think they have thee do very oft prove fools; and I, that am sure I lack thee, may pass for a wise man.] **For what says Quinapalus? 'Better a witty fool than a foolish wit.'** *(Enter OLIVIA with MALVOLIO)* **God bless thee, lady!**

50   **OLIVIA**   **Take the fool away.**

FESTE   **Do you not hear, fellows? Take away the lady.**

[OLIVIA   Go to, you're a dry fool! I'll no more of you. Besides, you grow dishonest.

FESTE   Two faults, madonna, that drink and good counsel will amend: for, give the dry fool drink, then is the fool not dry; bid the dishonest man mend himself -- if he mend, he is no longer dishonest; if he cannot, let the botcher mend him. Any thing that's

60   mended is but patched: virtue that transgresses is but patched with sin; and sin that amends is but patched with virtue. If that this simple syllogism will serve, so; if it will not, what remedy? As there is no true cuckold but calamity, so beauty's a flower. The lady bade take away the fool, therefore, I say again, take her away.]

OLIVIA   **Sir, I bade them take away you.**

FESTE   **Misprision in the highest degree!** [Lady, *cucullus non facit monachum*; that's as much to say as I wear not motley in my brain.] **Good madonna, give me leave to prove you a fool.**

70

OLIVIA   **Can you do it?**

FESTE   **Dexterously, good madonna.**

OLIVIA   **Make your proof.**

[FESTE   I must catechise you for it, madonna. Good my mouse of virtue, answer me.

80   OLIVIA   Well, sir, for want of other idleness, I'll bide your proof.]

FESTE   **Good madonna, why mournest thou?**

OLIVIA   **Good fool, for my brother's death.**

FESTE   **I think his soul is in hell, madonna.**

OLIVIA   **I know his soul is in heaven, fool.**

90   **FESTE**   **The more fool, madonna, to mourn for your brother's soul being in heaven. -- Take away the fool, gentlemen.**

OLIVIA   **What think you of this fool, Malvolio? Doth he not mend?**

[MALVOLIO   Yes, and shall do till the pangs of death shake him. Infirmity, that decays the wise, doth ever make the better fool.

FESTE   God send you, sir, a speedy infirmity, for the better increasing your folly!
100   Sir Toby will be sworn that I am no fox; but he will not pass his word for two pence that you are no fool.

OLIVIA   How say you to that, Malvolio?]

MALVOLIO   I marvel your ladyship takes delight in such a barren rascal. I saw him put down the other day with an ordinary fool that has no more brain than a stone. -- Look you now, he's out of his guard already. Unless you laugh and minister occasion to him, he is gagged. [I protest, I take these wise men -- that crow so at these set kind of
110   fools -- no better than the fools' zanies.]

OLIVIA   Oh, you are sick of self-love, Malvolio, and taste with a distempered appetite. [To be generous, guiltless and of free disposition, is to take those things for bird-bolts that you deem cannon-bullets. There is no slander in an allowed fool, though he do nothing but rail, nor no railing in a known discreet man, though he do nothing but reprove.]

FESTE   Now Mercury endue thee with leasing, for thou speakest well of fools!]

120   *Enter MARIA.*

MARIA   Madam, there is at the gate a young gentleman much desires to speak with you.

OLIVIA   From the Count Orsino, is it?

MARIA   I know not, madam. 'tis a fair young man, and well attended.

130   **OLIVIA   Who of my people hold him in delay?**

MARIA   Sir Toby, madam, your kinsman.

OLIVIA   Fetch him off, I pray you. He speaks nothing but madman, fie on him. *(Exit MARIA).* **Go you, Malvolio. If it be a suit from the Count, I am sick or not at home -- what you will, to dismiss it.** *(Exit MALVOLIO)* **Now you see, sir, how your fooling grows old, and people dislike it.**

140   [FESTE   Thou hast spoke for us, madonna, as if thy eldest son should be a fool,

whose skull Jove cram with brains, for -- here he comes -- one of thy kin has a most weak
pia mater.]

    Enter SIR TOBY.

OLIVIA	**By mine honour, half drunk. -- What is he at the gate,**
	cousin?

150

SIR TOBY	**A gentleman.**

OLIVIA	**A gentleman? What gentleman?**

SIR TOBY	**'Tis a gentle man here ... a plague o' these pickle-**
	herring ... *(To Feste)* **How now, sot?**

FESTE	**Good Sir Toby.**

OLIVIA	**Cousin, cousin, how have you come so early by this**
	lethargy?

160

SIR TOBY	**Lechery? I defy lechery. -- There's one at the gate.**

OLIVIA	**Ay, marry, what is he?**

SIR TOBY	**Let him be the devil, an he will, I care not. Give me**
	faith, say I. -- Well, it's all one. *(Exit)*

OLIVIA	**What's a drunken man like, fool?**

170   **FESTE**   **Like a drowned man, a fool and a madman: one
draught above heat makes him a fool; the second mads him; and a
third drowns him.**

OLIVIA	**Go thou and seek the coroner, and let him sit o' my**
	coz. For he's in the third degree of drink, he's drowned. Go, look
	after him.

FESTE	**He is but mad yet, madonna -- and the fool shall look**
	to the madman.

180

    Exit. Enter MALVOLIO.

MALVOLIO   **Madam, yond young fellow swears he will speak with
you. I told him you were sick -- he takes on him to understand so
much, and therefore comes to speak with you. I told him you were
asleep -- he seems to have a foreknowledge of that too, and
therefore comes to speak with you. What is to be said to him, lady?
He's fortified against any denial.**

190   **OLIVIA**   **Tell him he shall not speak with me.**

MALVOLIO   **He's been told so. And he says, he'll stand at your
door like a sheriff's post,** [and be the supporter to a bench,] **but he'll speak
with you.**

OLIVIA	**What kind o' man is he?**

MALVOLIO	**Why, of mankind.**

200   **OLIVIA**   **What manner of man?**

MALVOLIO   **Of very ill manner. He'll speak with you, will you or**

no.

OLIVIA   Of what personage and years is he?

MALVOLIO   Not yet old enough for a man, nor young enough for a
boy. [As a squash is before 'tis a peascod, or a cooling when 'tis almost an apple. 'Tis
with him in standing water -- between boy and man.] He is very well-favoured
210   and he speaks very shrewishly. One would think his mother's milk
were scarce out of him.

OLIVIA   Let him approach. Call in my gentlewoman.

MALVOLIO   Gentlewoman, my lady calls.

Exit. Enter MARIA.

OLIVIA   Give me my veil. Come, throw it o'er my face.
220   We'll once more hear Orsino's embassy.

Enter VIOLA [and ATTENDANTS].

VIOLA   The honourable lady of the house, which is she?

OLIVIA   Speak to me, I shall answer for her. Your will?

VIOLA   Most radiant, exquisite and unmatchable beauty ... I
pray you, tell me if this be the lady of the house, for I never saw
230   her. I would be loath to cast away my speech, for besides that it is
excellently well penned, I have taken great pains to con it. -- Good
beauties, let me sustain no scorn. [I am very 'countable, even to the least
sinister usage.]

OLIVIA   Whence came you, sir?

VIOLA   [I can say little more than I have studied, and that question's out of my
part.] Good gentle one, give me modest assurance if you be the lady
of the house, that I may proceed in my speech.
240
OLIVIA   Are you a comedian?

VIOLA   No, my profound heart. and yet [-- by the very fangs of malice
I swear --] I am not that I play. Are you the lady of the house?

OLIVIA   If I do not usurp myself, I am.

VIOLA   [Most certain, if you are she, you do usurp yourself. For what is yours to
bestow is not yours to reserve. But this is from my commission.] I will on with my
250   speech in your praise, and then show you the heart of my message.

OLIVIA   Come to what is important in't.   I forgive you the
praise.

VIOLA   Alas, I took great pains to study it, and 'tis poetical.

OLIVIA   It is the more like to be feigned. I pray you, keep it in.
I heard you were saucy at my gates ... [and allowed your approach rather to
wonder at you than to hear you.] If you be not mad, be gone. If you have
260   reason, be brief. ['Tis not that time of moon with me to make one in so skipping a
dialogue.]

MARIA   Will you hoist sail, sir? Here lies your way.

VIOLA No, good swabber, I am to hull here a little longer. [-- Some mollification for your giant, sweet lady.] **Tell me your mind. I am a messenger.**

270 **OLIVIA** Sure, you have some hideous matter to deliver, when the courtesy of it is so fearful. Speak your office.

VIOLA It alone concerns your ear. I bring no overture of war; [no taxation of homage; I hold the olive in my hand;] **my words are as full of peace as matter.**

OLIVIA Yet you began rudely. What are you? What would you?

VIOLA [The rudeness that hath appeared in me have I learned from my entertainment.] **What I am, and what I would, are as secret as**
280 **maidenhead: to your ears, divinity; to any other's, profanation.**

OLIVIA Give us the place alone, we will hear this divinity.
(Exeunt MARIA [and ATTENDANTS])
Now, sir, what is your text?

VIOLA Most sweet lady --

OLIVIA A comfortable doctrine, and much may be said of it. Where lies your text?
290

VIOLA In Orsino's bosom.

[OLIVIA In his bosom! In what chapter of his bosom?

VIOLA To answer by the method, in the first of his heart.]

OLIVIA O, I have read it. It is heresy. Have you no more to say?

300 **VIOLA** Good madam, let me see your face.

OLIVIA Have you any commission from your lord to negotiate with my face? [You are now out of your text.] **But we will draw the curtain and show you the picture ...** *(Unveils)* **Look you, sir,** [such a one I was this present:] **is't not well done?**

VIOLA Excellently done -- if God did all.

OLIVIA 'Tis in grain, sir, 'twill endure wind and weather.
310

VIOLA ['Tis beauty truly blent, whose red and white
Nature's own sweet and cunning hand laid on.]
**Lady, you are the cruellest she alive,
If you will lead these graces to the grave
And leave the world no copy.**

OLIVIA O, sir, I will not be so hard-hearted. I will give out divers schedules of my beauty. It shall be inventoried, and every particle and utensil labelled [to my will] as: *item*, two lips, indifferent
320 red; *item*, two grey eyes, with lids to them; *item*, one neck, one chin, and so forth. Were you sent hither to praise me?

VIOLA I see you what you are, you are too proud.
But, if you were the devil, you are fair.

My lord and master loves you. [O, such love
Could be but recompensed, though you were crowned
The nonpareil of beauty!]

330

OLIVIA How does he love me?

VIOLA With adorations, fertile tears,
With groans that thunder love, with sighs of fire.

OLIVIA Your lord does know my mind. I cannot love him.
Yet I suppose him virtuous, know him noble,
[Of great estate, of fresh and stainless youth;
In voices well divulged, free, learned and valiant;]
And in dimension and the shape of nature
A gracious person. But yet I cannot love him.

340 He might have took his answer long ago.

VIOLA If I did love you in my master's flame,
[With such a suffering, such a deadly life,]
In your denial I would find no sense,
I would not understand it.

OLIVIA Why, what would you?

VIOLA Make me a willow cabin at your gate,
350 And call upon my soul within the house;
Write loyal cantons of contemnèd love
And sing them loud even in the dead of night;
Halloo your name to the reverberate hills
And make the babbling gossip of the air
Cry out 'Olivia!' [O, You should not rest
Between the elements of air and earth,
But you should pity me!]

OLIVIA You might do much. What is your parentage?

360

VIOLA Above my fortunes, yet my state is well.
I am a gentleman.

OLIVIA Get you to your lord.
I cannot love him. Let him send no more –
Unless, perchance, you come to me again
To tell me how he takes it. Fare you well.
I thank you for your pains. – Spend this for me.

370 **VIOLA** I am no fee'd post, lady, keep your purse.
My master, not myself, lacks recompense.
[Love make his heart of flint that you shall love;
And let your fervor, like my master's, be
Placed in contempt. Farewell, fair cruelty.] *(Exit)*

OLIVIA "What is your parentage?"
"Above my fortunes, yet my state is well.
I am a gentleman." I'll be sworn thou art.
[Thy tongue, thy face, thy limbs, actions and spirit,
380 Do give thee five-fold blazon. Not too fast ... soft, soft!
Unless the master were the man.] **How now?**

23

Even so quickly may one catch the plague?
Methinks I feel this youth's perfections
With an invisible and subtle stealth
To creep in at mine eyes ... Well, let it be.
What ho, Malvolio!

Enter MALVOLIO.

390   **MALVOLIO**   Here, madam, at your service.

OLIVIA   Run after that same peevish messenger,
The County's man. He left this ring behind him,
Would I or not. Tell him I'll none of it.
Desire him not to flatter with his lord,
Nor hold him up with hopes, I am not for him.
If that the youth will come this way tomorrow,
I'll give him reasons for't. Hie thee, Malvolio.

400   **MALVOLIO**   Madam, I will.   *(Exit)*

OLIVIA   [I do I know not what, and fear to find
Mine eye too great a flatterer for my mind.]
Fate, show thy force. Ourselves we do not owe.
What is decreed must be, and be this so.   *(Exit)*

ACT TWO
Scene1   *[Near the coast.]*
Enter ANTONIO and SEBASTIAN.

ANTONIO   Will you stay no longer? Nor will you not that I go with you?

SEBASTIAN   By your patience, no. My stars shine darkly over me.
The malignancy of my fate might perhaps distemper yours;
10   [therefore I shall crave of you your leave that I may bear my evils alone;] it were a
bad recompense for your love[, to lay any of them on you].

ANTONIO   Let me yet know of you whither you are bound.

SEBASTIAN   No, sooth, sir, [my determinate voyage is mere extravagancy;] but I
perceive in you so excellent a touch of modesty, that [you will not
extort from me what I am willing to keep in; therefore] it charges me in manners
the rather to express myself. You must know of me then, Antonio,
my name is Sebastian, which I called Roderigo. My father [was that
20   Sebastian of Messaline, whom I know you have heard of. He] left behind him
myself and a sister, both born in an hour. If the heavens had been
pleased, would we had so ended, but you, sir, altered that. For
some hour before you took me from the breach of the sea was my
sister drowned.

ANTONIO   Alas the day!

SEBASTIAN   A lady, sir – though it was said she much resembled
me – was yet of many accounted beautiful; [but, though I could not with

30 such estimable wonder over-far believe that, yet thus far I will boldly publish her:] **she bore a mind that envy could not but call fair. She is drowned already, sir, with salt water, though I seem to drown her remembrance again with more.**

[ANTONIO   Pardon me, sir, your bad entertainment.

SEBASTIAN   O good Antonio, forgive me your trouble.]

ANTONIO   If you will not murder me for my love, let me be your
40 **servant.**

SEBASTIAN If you will not undo what you have done, that is, kill him whom you have recovered, desire it not. [Fare ye well at once. My bosom is full of kindness, and I am yet so near the manners of my mother, that upon the least occasion more mine eyes will tell tales of me.] **I am bound to the Count Orsino's court, farewell.**   *(Exit)*

ANTONIO   The gentleness of all the gods go with thee.
I have many enemies in Orsino's court,
50 **Else would I very shortly see thee there ...**
But, come what may, I do adore thee so,
That danger shall seem sport, and I will go.   *(Exit)*

Scene 2   *[A street near Olivia's house.]*
Enter VIOLA, MALVOLIO following.

MALVOLIO   Were not you even now with the Countess Olivia?

VIOLA   Even now, sir. On a moderate pace I have since arrived but hither.

MALVOLIO She returns this ring to you, sir. You might have
10 **saved me my pains, to have taken it away yourself. She adds, moreover, that you should put your lord into a desperate assurance she will none of him. And one thing more: that you be never so hardy to come again in his affairs, unless it be to report your lord's taking of this. Receive it so.**

VIOLA   She took the ring of me. I'll none of it.

MALVOLIO Come, sir, you peevishly threw it to her. And her will is, it should be so returned. If it be worth stooping for, there it lies
20 **in your eye. If not, be it his that finds it.**   *(Exit)*

VIOLA   I left no ring with her. What means this lady?
Fortune forbid my outside have not charmed her.
She made good view of me ... indeed, so much,
That sure methought her eyes had lost her tongue ...
[For she did speak in starts distractedly.
She loves me, sure. The cunning of her passion
Invites me in this churlish messenger.
None of my lord's ring? Why, he sent her none.]
30 **I am the man. If it be so, as 'tis,**
Poor lady, she were better love a dream.
[Disguise, I see, thou art a wickedness,

25

Wherein the pregnant enemy does much.
How easy is it for the proper-false
In women's waxen hearts to set their forms!
Alas, our frailty is the cause, not we,
For such as we are made of, such we be.
How will this fadge? My master loves her dearly;
And I, poor monster, fond as much on him;
40   And she, mistaken, seems to dote on me.]
What will become of this? As I am man,
My state is desperate for my master's love;
As I am woman – now alas the day –
What thriftless sighs shall poor Olivia breathe?
O time, thou must untangle this, not I.
It is too hard a knot for me to untie.

                                                        (Exit)

Scene 3.   *[A room in Olivia's house.]*
                  Enter SIR TOBY and SIR ANDREW.

SIR TOBY   **Approach, Sir Andrew. Not to be abed after midnight is to be up betimes.** [And *'diluculo surgere'*, thou know'st …]

ANDREW   [Nay, my troth, I know not. But] **I know to be up late is to be up late.**

10   **SIR TOBY**   **A false conclusion. I hate it as an unfilled can. To be up after midnight and to go to bed then, is early; so that to go to bed after midnight is to go to bed betimes. Does not our life consist of the four elements?**

ANDREW   **Faith, so they say, but I think it rather consists of eating and drinking.**

SIR TOBY   **Thou'rt a scholar. Let us therefore eat and drink.**
20   **Marian, I say! A stoup of wine!**

      Enter FESTE.

ANDREW   **Here comes the fool, i' faith.**

FESTE   **How now, my hearts?** [Did you never see the picture of 'we three'?]

SIR TOBY   **Welcome, ass. Now let's have a catch.**

30   **ANDREW**   **By my troth, the fool has an excellent breast. I had rather than forty shillings I had such a leg, and so sweet a breath to sing, as the fool has. In sooth, thou wast in very gracious fooling last night:** [when thou spokest of Pigrogromitus, of the Vapians passing the equinoctial of Queubus, 'twas very good, i' faith.] **I sent thee sixpence for thy leman. Hadst it?**

FESTE   **I did impeticos thy gratillity.** [For Malvolio's nose is no whipstock. My lady has a white hand, and the Myrmidons are no bottle-ale houses.]

40   **ANDREW**   **Excellent!** [Why, this is the best fooling, when all is done.] **Now, a song.**

SIR TOBY   **Come on, there is sixpence for you, let's l**

[ANDREW   There's a testril of me too. If one knight give a --

FESTE   Would you have a love-song, or a song of good life?

50

SIR TOBY   A love-song, a love-song.

ANDREW   Ay, ay, I care not for good life.

FESTE *(Sings)*   O mistress mine, where are you roaming?
O, stay and hear, your true love's coming,
That can sing both high and low.
Trip no further, pretty sweeting,
Journeys end in lovers meeting,
Every wise man's son doth know.

60   ANDREW   Excellent good, i' faith.

SIR TOBY   Good, good.]

FESTE *(Sings)*   **What is love? 'Tis not hereafter.
Present mirth hath present laughter.
What's to come is still unsure.
In delay there lies no plenty;
Then come kiss me, sweet and twenty,
Youth's a stuff will not endure.**

70

ANDREW   **A mellifluous voice, as I am true knight.**

SIR TOBY   **A contagious breath.**

[ANDREW   Very sweet and contagious, i' faith.

SIR TOBY   To hear by the nose, it is dulcet in contagion. But shall we make the welkin dance indeed? Shall we rouse the night-owl in a catch that will draw three souls out of one weaver? Shall we do that?

80

ANDREW   An you love me, let's do't. I am dog at a catch.

FESTE   By'r lady, sir, and some dogs will catch well.

ANDREW   Most certain. Let our catch be 'Thou Knave.'

FESTE   'Hold thy peace, thou knave,' knight? I shall be constrained in't to call thee knave, knight.

90   ANDREW   'Tis not the first time I have constrained one to call me knave. Begin, fool. It begins 'Hold thy Peace.'

FESTE   I shall never begin if I hold my peace.

ANDREW   Good, i' faith. Come, begin.

Catch sung.] *Enter MARIA.*

MARIA   **What a caterwauling do you keep here! If my lady**
100   **have not called up her steward Malvolio and bid him turn you out of doors, never trust me.**

SIR TOBY   [My lady's a Cataian, we are politicians, Malvolio's a Peg-o'-Ramsey, and "Three merry men be we." Am not I consanguineous? Am I not of her blood? Tilly-vally, lady!] *(Sings)*   **'There dwelt a man in Babylon, lady, lady!'**

FESTE   **Beshrew me, the knight's in admirable fooling.**

110   **ANDREW**   **Ay, he does well enough if he be disposed, and so do I too. He does it with a better grace, but I do it more natural.**

SIR TOBY *(Sings)*   **'O' the twelfth day of December'** --

MARIA   **For the love o' God, peace!**

Enter MALVOLIO.

120   **MALVOLIO**   **My masters, are you mad, or what are you? Have ye no wit, manners, nor honesty, but to gabble like tinkers at this time of night?** [Do ye make an alehouse of my lady's house, that ye squeak out your coziers' catches without any mitigation or remorse of voice?] **Is there no respect of place, persons, nor time in you?**

SIR TOBY   **We did keep time, sir -- in our catches. Sneck up!**

130   **MALVOLIO**   **Sir Toby, I must be round with you. My lady bade me tell you that, though she harbours you as her kinsman, she's nothing allied to your disorders. If you can separate yourself and your misdemeanours, you are welcome to the house; if not, an it would please you to take leave of her, she is very willing to bid you farewell.**

SIR TOBY *(Sings)* **'Farewell, dear heart, since I must needs be gone.'**

MARIA   **Nay, good Sir Toby ...**

[FESTE *(Sings)*   'His eyes do show his days are almost done.'

140   MALVOLIO   Is't even so?

SIR TOBY *(Sings)*   'But I will never die.'

FESTE *(Sings)*   'Sir Toby, there you lie.'

MALVOLIO   This is much credit to you.

SIR TOBY *(Sings)*   'Shall I bid him go?'

150   FESTE *(Sings)*   'What an if you do?'

SIR TOBY *(Sings)*   'Shall I bid him go, and spare not?'

FESTE *(Sings)*   'O no, no, no, no, you dare not.']

SIR TOBY   [Out o' tune, sir? Ye lie.] **Art any more than a steward? Dost thou think, because thou art virtuous, there shall be no more cakes and ale?**

160   [FESTE   Yes, by Saint Anne, and ginger shall be hot i' the mouth too.]

SIR TOBY   [Thou'rt i' the right. Go, sir, rub your chain with crumbs.] **A stoup of wine, Maria!**

MALVOLIO   **Mistress Mary, if you prized my lady's favour at any thing more than contempt, you would not give means for this uncivil rule. She shall know of it, by this hand.**   *(Exit)*

MARIA   Go shake your ears.

170 **ANDREW**   'Twere as good a deed as to drink when a man's a-hungry, to challenge him the field, and then to break promise with him and make a fool of him.

SIR TOBY   Do 't, knight. I'll write thee a challenge. Or I'll deliver thy indignation to him by word of mouth.

MARIA   Sweet Sir Toby, be patient for tonight Since the youth of the Count's was today with thy lady, she is much out of quiet. For Monsieur Malvolio, let me alone with him. If I do not
180 **gull him** [into a nayword, and make him a common recreation], **do not think I have wit enough to lie straight in my bed.** [I know I can do it.]

SIR TOBY   Possess us, possess us, tell us something of him.

MARIA   Marry, sir, sometimes he is a kind of Puritan.

ANDREW   O, if I thought that I'd beat him like a dog.

SIR TOBY   What, for being a Puritan? Thy exquisite reason, dear
190 knight?

ANDREW   I have no exquisite reason for't, but I have reason good enough.

MARIA   The devil a Puritan that he is, or anything constantly, but a time-pleaser; an affectated ass, [that cons state without book and utters it by great swathes; the best persuaded of himself,] so crammed -- as he thinks -- with excellencies, that it is his grounds of faith that all that look on him love him. And on that vice in him will my
200 revenge find notable cause to work.

SIR TOBY   What wilt thou do?

MARIA   I will drop in his way some obscure epistles of love; wherein, by the colour of his beard, the shape of his leg, the manner of his gait, the expressure of his eye, forehead, and complexion, he shall find himself most feelingly personated. I can write very like my lady your niece. [On a forgotten matter we can hardly make distinction of our hands.]
210

SIR TOBY   Excellent! I smell a device.

ANDREW   I have't in my nose too.

SIR TOBY   He shall think, by the letters that thou wilt drop, that they come from my niece, and that she's in love with him.

MARIA   My purpose is, indeed, a horse of that colour.

220 [**ANDREW**   And your horse now would make him an ass.

MARIA   Ass, I doubt not.]

ANDREW   O, 'twill be admirable!

MARIA   Sport royal, I warrant you. I know my physic will work with him. I will plant you two, and let the fool make a third, where he shall find the letter. Observe his construction of it. For

29

230 **this night, to bed, and dream on the event. Farewell.** *(Exit)*

[SIR TOBY   Good night, Penthesilea.]

ANDREW   **Before me, she's a good wench.**

SIR TOBY   **She's a beagle, true-bred, and one that adores me. --
What o' that?**

ANDREW   **I was adored once too.**

240 **SIR TOBY**   **Let's to bed, knight. Thou hadst need send for more
money.**

ANDREW   **If I cannot recover your niece, I am a foul way out.**

[SIR TOBY   Send for money, knight. If thou hast her not i' the end, call me Cut.

ANDREW   If I do not, never trust me. Take it how you will.]

SIR TOBY   **Come, come, I'll go burn some sack. 'Tis too late to go**
250 **to bed now. Come, knight, come, knight.**   *(Exeunt)*

Scene 4   *[In Duke Orsino's palace.]*
        Enter ORSINO with VIOLA*[, CURIO and others]*.

[ORSINO   Give me some music. Now, good morrow, friends.
Now, good Cesario, but that piece of song,
That old and antique song we heard last night.
Methought it did relieve my passion much.
More than light airs and recollected terms
Of these most brisk and giddy-pacèd times.]
10 Come, but one verse.

CURIO   He is not here, so please your lordship that should sing it.

ORSINO   Who was it?

CURIO   Feste the jester, my lord, a fool that the lady Olivia's father took much
delight in. He is about the house.

20 ORSINO   Seek him out, and play the tune the while.

    Exit CURIO.] Music plays.

ORSINO   **Come hither, boy.** [If ever thou shalt love,
In the sweet pangs of it remember me.
For such as I am, all true lovers are:
Unstaid and skittish in all motions else,
Save in the constant image of the creature
That is beloved.] **How dost thou like this tune?**

30 **VIOLA**   **It gives a very echo to the seat
Where love is throned.**

ORSINO   **Thou dost speak masterly.
My life upon't, young though thou art, thine eye
Hath stayed upon some favour that it loves.
Hath it not, boy?**

VIOLA   A little, by your favour.

40   ORSINO   What kind of woman is't?

VIOLA   Of your complexion.

ORSINO   She is not worth thee then. What years, i' faith?

VIOLA   About your years, my lord.

ORSINO   Too old by heaven. Let still the woman take
An elder than herself: so wears she to him,
50   So sways she level in her husband's heart;
For, boy, however we do praise ourselves,
Our fancies are more giddy and unfirm,
More longing, wavering, sooner lost and worn,
Than women's are.

VIOLA   I think it well, my lord.

ORSINO   Then let thy love be younger than thyself,
Or thy affection cannot hold the bent;
60   For women are as roses, whose fair flower
Being once displayed, doth fall that very hour.

VIOLA   And so they are. Alas, that they are so:
To die, even when they to perfection grow.

Enter [CURIO and] FESTE.

ORSINO   O, fellow, come, the song we had last night.
Mark it, Cesario, it is old and plain.
70   [The spinsters and the knitters in the sun
And the free maids that weave their thread with bones
Do use to chant it. It is silly sooth,
And dallies with the innocence of love,
Like the old age.

FESTE   Are you ready, sir?

ORSINO   Ay, prithee, sing.]

80   *Music.*

                     [Song.

FESTE   Come away, come away, death,
          And in sad cypress let me be laid.
   Fly away, fly away breath,
          I am slain by a fair cruel maid.
   My shroud of white, stuck all with yew,
          O, prepare it.
   My part of death, no one so true
90   Did share it.

   Not a flower, not a flower sweet
          On my black coffin let there be strewn.
   Not a friend, not a friend greet
          My poor corpse, where my bones shall be thrown.

A thousand thousand sighs to save,
Lay me, O, where
Sad true lover never find my grave,
To weep there.

100

ORSINO   There's for thy pains.

FESTE   No pains, sir, I take pleasure in singing, sir.

ORSINO   I'll pay thy pleasure then.

FESTE   Truly, sir, and pleasure will be paid, one time or another.

ORSINO   Give me now leave to leave thee.
110

FESTE   Now, the melancholy god protect thee ... and the tailor make thy
doublet of changeable taffeta, for thy mind is a very opal. I would have men of such
constancy put to sea, that their business might be every thing and their intent every
where; for that's it that always makes a good voyage of nothing ... Farewell.]   (*Exit*)

ORSINO   [Let all the rest give place. *(CURIO and ATTENDANTS retire)]*
                              Once more, Cesario,
Get thee to yond same sovereign cruelty.
[Tell her: my love, more noble than the world,
120   Prizes not quantity of dirty lands.]
The parts that fortune hath bestowed upon her,
Tell her, I hold as giddily as fortune.
[But 'tis that miracle and queen of gems
That nature pranks her in attracts my soul.]

VIOLA   **But if she cannot love you, sir?**

ORSINO   **I cannot be so answered.**

130 **VIOLA**   **Sooth, but you must.**
Say that some lady, as perhaps there is,
Hath for your love as great a pang of heart
As you have for Olivia. You cannot love her,
You tell her so. Must she not then be answered?

ORSINO   **There is no woman's sides**
Can bide the beating of so strong a passion
As love doth give my heart; no woman's heart
So big, to hold so much. [They lack retention.
140   Alas, their love may be called appetite:
No motion of the liver, but the palate,
That suffers surfeit, cloyment and revolt.
But mine is all as hungry as the sea,
And can digest as much] **Make no compare**
Between that love a woman can bear me
And that I owe Olivia.

VIOLA   **Ay, but I know --**

150 **ORSINO**   **What dost thou know?**

VIOLA   **Too well what love women to men may owe.**
In faith, they are as true of heart as we.
My father had a daughter loved a man,

As it might be, perhaps, were I a woman,
I should your lordship.

ORSINO   And what's her history?

160   **VIOLA**   A blank, my lord. She never told her love,
But let concealment, like a worm i' the bud,
Feed on her damask cheek. She pined in thought ...
[And with a green and yellow melancholy
She sat like patience on a monument,
Smiling at grief. Was not this love indeed?]
We men may say more, swear more, but indeed
Our shows are more than will; for still we prove
Much in our vows, but little in our love.

170   **ORSINO**   But died thy sister of her love, my boy?

VIOLA   I am all the daughters of my father's house,
And all the brothers too, and yet I know not.
Sir, shall I to this lady?

ORSINO   Ay, that's the theme.
To her in haste, give her this jewel. Say
My love can give no place, bide no denay.   *(Exeunt)*

Scene 5   *[Olivia's garden.]*
              Enter SIR TOBY, SIR ANDREW and FABIAN.

[SIR TOBY   Come thy ways, Signior Fabian.]

FABIAN   [Nay, I'll come.] **If I lose a scruple of this sport, let me be
boiled to death with melancholy.**

SIR TOBY   Wouldst thou not be glad to have the niggardly
10   rascally sheep-biter come by some notable shame?

FABIAN   I would exult, man. You know, he brought me out o'
favour with my lady about a bear-baiting here.

SIR TOBY   [To anger him we'll have the bear again; and...] **We will fool him
black and blue, shall we not, Sir Andrew?**

ANDREW   An we do not, it is pity of our lives.

20   **SIR TOBY**   Here comes the little villain. *(Enter MARIA)* How now,
my metal of India?

MARIA   Get ye all three into the box-tree. Malvolio's coming
down this walk. He has been yonder in the sun practising behaviour to his own shadow this half hour. Observe him, for the love of
mockery, for I know this letter will make a contemplative idiot of
him. [Close, in the name of jesting!] **Lie thou there,** *(throws down a letter)*
for here comes the trout that must be caught with tickling.   *(Exit)*

30   *Enter MALVOLIO.*

MALVOLIO   'Tis but fortune, all is fortune ... Maria once told me
she did affect me, and I have heard herself come thus near: that,

should she fancy, it should be one of my complexion. Besides, she uses me with a more exalted respect than anyone else that follows her. What should I think on't?

SIR TOBY   Here's an overweening rogue.

40   FABIAN   [O, peace! Contemplation makes a rare turkey-cock of him.] **How he jets under his advanced plumes!**

ANDREW   **'S light, I could so beat the rogue!**

SIR TOBY   **Peace, I say.**

MALVOLIO   **To be Count Malvolio!**

50   SIR TOBY   **Ah, rogue!**

ANDREW   **Pistol him, pistol him.**

SIR TOBY   **Peace, peace!**

[MALVOLIO   There is example for't: the lady of the Strachy married the yeoman of the wardrobe.

ANDREW   Fie on him, Jezebel!

60   FABIAN   O, peace! Now he's deeply in. Look how imagination blows him.]

MALVOLIO   **Having been three months married to her, sitting in my state —**

[SIR TOBY   O, for a stone-bow, to hit him in the eye!]

MALVOLIO   [Calling my officers about me, in my branched velvet gown;] **having come from a day-bed where I have left Olivia sleeping —**

70   SIR TOBY   **Fire and brimstone!**

FABIAN   **O, peace, peace!**

MALVOLIO   **And then** [to have the humour of state; and after a demure travel of regard,] **telling them I know my place as I would they should do theirs, to ask for my kinsman Toby —**

SIR TOBY   **Bolts and shackles!**

80   FABIAN   **O peace, peace, peace, now, now!**

MALVOLIO   **Seven of my people, with an obedient start, make out for him. I frown the while, and perchance wind up my watch, or play with my... some rich jewel. Toby approaches, curtsies there to me -**

SIR TOBY   **Shall this fellow live?**

[FABIAN   Though our silence be drawn from us with cars, yet peace.]

90   MALVOLIO   **I extend my hand to him thus, quenching my familiar smile with an austere regard of control —**

[SIR TOBY   And does not Toby take you a blow o' the lips then?]

MALVOLIO   **Saying, "Cousin Toby, my fortunes having cast me on**

34

your niece, give me this prerogative of speech ..."

100	**SIR TOBY**	What, what?
	MALVOLIO	"You must amend your drunkenness."
	SIR TOBY	Out, scab!
	FABIAN	Nay, patience, or we break the sinews of our plot.

MALVOLIO "Besides, you waste the treasure of your time with a foolish knight —"

110 **ANDREW** That's me, I warrant you.

MALVOLIO "One Sir Andrew."

ANDREW I knew 'twas I, for many do call me fool.

MALVOLIO What employment have we here? *(Takes up the letter)*

FABIAN Now is the woodcock near the gin.

120 [SIR TOBY   O, peace and the spirit of humours intimate reading aloud to him!]

MALVOLIO By my life, this is my lady's hand these be her very C's, her U's and her T's and thus makes she her great P's. It is, in contempt of question, her hand.

ANDREW Her C's, her U's and her T's ... why that?

MALVOLIO *(Reads)* 'To the unknown beloved, this, and my good wishes.' Her very phrases! By your leave, wax ... soft ... [And the 130 impressure her Lucrece, with which she uses to seal -- 'tis my lady. To whom should this be?]

FABIAN This wins him, liver and all.

MALVOLIO *(Reads)*   'Jove knows I love,
                    But who?
             Lips, do not move –
              No man must know.'
'No man must know ...' [What follows? The numbers altered! 'No man must 140 know'...] If this should be thee, Malvolio?

SIR TOBY Marry, hang thee, brock!

MALVOLIO *(Reads)*   'I may command where I adore;
             But silence, like a Lucrece knife,
          With bloodless stroke my heart doth gore.
             M. O. A. I. doth sway my life.'

150 **FABIAN** A fustian riddle!

SIR TOBY Excellent wench, say I.

MALVOLIO 'M. O. A. I. doth sway my life.' Nay, but first let me see, let me see, let me see ...

FABIAN What dish o' poison has she dressed him!

[SIR TOBY   And with what wing the staniel checks at it!]

35

160 **MALVOLIO 'I may command where I adore.' Why, she may command me, I serve her, she is my lady ...** [Why, this is evident to any formal capacity] **... there is no obstruction in this. And the end – what should that alphabetical position portend? If I could make that resemble something in me ... softly ... 'M. O. A. I ...'**

[SIR TOBY   O ay, make up that. He is now at a cold scent.

FABIAN   Sowter will cry upon't for all this, though it be as rank as a fox.]

170 **MALVOLIO 'M' ... Malvolio! M, why, that begins my name.**

FABIAN   Did not I say he would work it out? The cur is excellent at faults.

MALVOLIO M ... but then there is no consonancy in the sequel. [That suffers under probation.] **'A' should follow, but 'O' does.**

FABIAN   And 'Oh' shall end, I hope!

180 **SIR TOBY   Ay, or I'll cudgel him, and make him cry Oh!**

[MALVOLIO   And then 'I' comes behind.

FABIAN   Ay, an you had any eye behind you, you might see more detraction at your heels than fortunes before you.]

MALVOLIO M. O. A. I ... this simulation is not as the former. And yet[, to crush this a little, it would bow to me, for] **every one of these letters are in my name ... Soft, here follows prose.** *(Reads)* **'If this fall into**
190 **thy hand, revolve. In my stars I am above thee, but be not afraid of greatness. Some are born great, some achieve greatness, and some have greatness thrust upon 'em. Thy Fates open their hands.** [Let thy blood and spirit embrace them; and, to inure thyself to what thou art like to be, cast thy humble slough and appear fresh.] **Be opposite with a kinsman, surly with servants.** [Let thy tongue tang arguments of state, put thyself into the trick of singularity.] **She thus advises thee that sighs for thee. Remember who commended thy yellow stockings, and wished to see thee ever cross-gartered. I say, remember. Go to, thou art made, if thou desirest to be so. If not, let me see thee a steward still, the fellow**
200 **of servants, and not worthy to touch Fortune's fingers. Farewell. She that would alter services with thee.**   [The Fortunate-Unhappy.' Daylight and champian discovers not more!] **This is open! I will be proud, I will read politic authors, I will baffle Sir Toby.** [I will wash off gross acquaintance, I will be *point-de-vice* the very man.] **I do not now fool myself, to let imagination jade me, for every reason excites to this, that my lady loves me. She did commend my yellow stockings of late, she did praise my leg being cross-gartered; and in this she manifests herself to my love ...** [and with a kind of injunction drives me to these habits of her liking. I thank my stars I am happy. I will be strange, stout, in yellow stockings, and cross-
210 gartered, even with the swiftness of putting on.] **Jove and my stars be praised! Here is yet a postscript...** *(Reads)* **'Thou canst not choose but know who I am. If thou entertainest my love, let it appear in thy smiling. Thy smiles become thee well; therefore in my presence still smile, dear my sweet, I prithee.' – Jove, I thank thee! I will smile. I will do everything that thou wilt have me.**   *(Exit)*

FABIAN   I will not give my part of this sport for a pension of thousands [to be paid from the Sophy].

220 SIR TOBY   I could marry this wench for this device.

ANDREW   So could I too.

SIR TOBY   And ask no other dowry with her but such another jest.

ANDREW   Nor I neither.

230 FABIAN   Here comes my noble gull-catcher.

Enter MARIA.

SIR TOBY   Wilt thou set thy foot o' my neck?

ANDREW   Or o' mine either?

[SIR TOBY   Shall I play my freedom at tray-trip, and become thy bond-slave?

240 ANDREW   I' faith, or I either?]

SIR TOBY   Why, thou hast put him in such a dream, that when the image of it leaves him he must run mad.

MARIA   Nay, but say true, does it work upon him?

SIR TOBY   Like *aqua vitae* with a midwife.

MARIA   If you will then see the fruits of the sport, mark his first approach before my lady.   He will come to her in yellow 250 stockings (and 'tis a colour she abhors) and cross-gartered (a fashion she detests).   And he will smile upon her, which will now be so unsuitable to her disposition, being addicted to a melancholy as she is, that it cannot but turn him into a notable contempt.   If you will see it, follow me.

SIR TOBY   To the gates of Tartar, thou most excellent devil of wit!

ANDREW   I'll make one too.   *(Exeunt)*

ACT THREE
Scene 1   *[Olivia's garden.]*
Enter VIOLA and FESTE with a tabour.

VIOLA   Save thee, friend — and thy music.   Dost thou live by thy tabour?

FESTE   No, sir, I live by the church.

10 VIOLA   Art thou a churchman?

FESTE   No such matter, sir.   I do live by the church, for I do live at my house, and my house doth stand by the church.

VIOLA **So thou mayst say, the king lies by a beggar, if a beggar dwell near him.** [Or the church stands by thy tabour, if thy tabour stand by the church.]

20 **FESTE** **You have said, sir!** [To see this age! A sentence is but a cheveril glove to a good wit -- how quickly the wrong side may be turned outward.]

VIOLA **Nay, that's certain.** [They that dally nicely with words may quickly make them wanton.

FESTE I would, therefore, my sister had had no name, sir.

VIOLA Why, man?

30 FESTE Why, sir, her name's a word, and to dally with that word might make my sister wanton. But indeed words are very rascals since bonds disgraced them.

VIOLA Thy reason, man?]

FESTE **Troth, sir,** [I can yield you none without words; and] **words are grown so false, I am loath to prove reason with them.**

VIOLA **I warrant thou art a merry fellow** – [and carest for nothing.

40 FESTE Not so, sir, I do care for something. But in my conscience, sir, I do not care for you. If that be to care for nothing, sir, I would it would make you invisible.]

VIOLA **Art not thou the Lady Olivia's fool?**

FESTE **No, indeed, sir.** [The Lady Olivia has no folly.] **She will keep no fool, sir, till she be married. And fools are as like husbands as pilchards are to herrings – the husband's the bigger. I am indeed not her fool, but her corrupter of words.**

50 **VIOLA** **I saw thee late at the Count Orsino's.**

FESTE [Foolery, sir, does walk about the orb like the sun, it shines everywhere.] **I would be sorry, sir, but the fool should be as oft with your master as with my mistress. I think I saw your wisdom there ...**

VIOLA **Nay, an thou pass upon me, I'll no more with thee. Hold, there's expenses for thee.**

60 **FESTE** **Now Jove, in his next commodity of hair, send thee a beard!**

VIOLA **By my troth, I'll tell thee, I am almost sick for one –** *(aside)* **though I would not have it grow on** *my* **chin. – Is thy lady within?**

FESTE **Would not a pair of these have bred, sir?**

[VIOLA Yes, being kept together and put to use.

70 FESTE I would play Lord Pandarus of Phrygia, sir, to bring a Cressida to this Troilus.]

VIOLA **I understand you, sir, 'tis well begged.** *(Gives another coin)*

FESTE [The matter, I hope, is not great, sir, begging but a beggar. Cressida was a beggar.] **My lady is within, sir. I will construe to them come. Who you are and what you would are out of** might say 'element', but the word is over-worn.

80 **VIOLA**   **This fellow is wise enough to play the foc**
And to do that well craves a kind of wit.
He must observe their mood on whom he jests,
The quality of persons, and the time ...
[And, like the haggard, check at every feather
That comes before his eye. This is a practice]
As full of labour as a wise man's art;
For folly that he wisely shows is fit;
But wise men, folly-fall'n, quite taint their wit.

90   *Enter SIR TOBY and SIR ANDREW.*

SIR TOBY   Save you, gentleman.

VIOLA   And you, sir.

ANDREW   *Dieu vous garde, monsieur.*

VIOLA   *Et vous aussi. Votre serviteur.*

100 **ANDREW**   I hope, sir, you are. And I am yours.

SIR TOBY   **Will you encounter the house? My niece is desirous you should enter, if your trade be to her.**

VIOLA   **I am bound to your niece, sir. I mean, she is the list of my voyage.**

[SIR TOBY   Taste your legs, sir, put them to motion.

110 VIOLA   My legs do better understand me, sir, than I understand what you mean by bidding me taste my legs.

SIR TOBY   I mean, to go, sir, to enter.]

VIOLA   [I will answer you with gait and entrance.] **But we are prevented.**
(Enter OLIVIA and [Gentlewoman] MARIA).
Most excellent accomplished lady, the heavens rain odours on you!

120 **ANDREW**   **That youth's a rare courtier. "Rain odours" – well!**

VIOLA   **My matter hath no voice, lady, but to your own most pregnant and vouchsafed ear.**

ANDREW   **"Odours," "pregnant" and "vouchsafed"!** [I'll get 'em all three all ready.]

OLIVIA   **Let the garden door be shut, and leave me to my hearing.** *(Exeunt SIR TOBY, SIR ANDREW and MARIA)* **Give me your hand, sir.**

130 **VIOLA**   **My duty, madam, and most humble service.**

OLIVIA   **What is your name?**

VIOLA   **Cesario is your servant's name, fair princess.**

OLIVIA   [My servant, sir! 'Twas never merry world
Since lowly feigning was called compliment.]
You're servant to the Count Orsino, youth.

140

[VIOLA   And he is yours, and his must needs be yours --
Your servant's servant is *your* servant, madam.

OLIVIA   For him, I think not on him. For his thoughts,
Would they were blanks rather than filled with me.

**VIOLA   Madam, I come to whet your gentle thoughts
On his behalf.**

150   **OLIVIA**   [O, by your leave, I pray you,]
**I bade you never speak again of him.
But, would you undertake another suit,
I had rather hear you to solicit that
Than music from the spheres.**

VIOLA   Dear lady --

**OLIVIA   Give me leave, beseech you ... I did send,
After the last enchantment you did here,**
160   **A ring in chase of you. So did I abuse
Myself, my servant and, I fear me, you.**
[Under your hard construction must I sit,
To force that on you in a shameful cunning,
Which you knew none of yours. What might you think?
Have you not set mine honour at the stake
And baited it with all the unmuzzled thoughts
That tyrannous heart can think? To one of your receiving
Enough is shown. A cypress, not a bosom,
Hides my heart.] **So, let me hear you speak.**

170   **VIOLA   I pity you.**

[OLIVIA   That's a degree to love.

VIOLA   No, not a grece. For 'tis a vulgar proof,
That very oft we pity enemies.]

**OLIVIA   Why, then, methinks 'tis time to smile again.
O, world, how apt the poor are to be proud!**
180   [If one should be a prey, how much the better
To fall before the lion than the wolf]   *(Clock strikes)*
**The clock upbraids me with the waste of time.
Be not afraid, good youth, I will not have you --
And yet, when wit and youth is come to harvest,
Your wife is like to reap a proper man.
There lies your way, due west.**

**VIOLA   Then westward ho!
Grace and good disposition attend your ladyship.**
190   **You'll nothing, madam, to my lord by me?**

**OLIVIA   Stay ...
I prithee, tell me what thou think'st of me.**

VIOLA   **That you do think you are not what you a**

OLIVIA   **If I think so, I think the same of you.**

200 VIOLA   **Then think you right. I am not what I am**

OLIVIA   **I would you were as I would have you be.**

VIOLA   **Would it be better, madam, than I am?**
I wish it might, for now I am your fool.

OLIVIA   *(Aside)* **O, what a deal of scorn looks beautiful**
In the contempt and anger of his lip!
A murderous guilt shows not itself more soon
Than love that would seem hid. Love's night is noon.
210 **Cesario, by the roses of the spring,**
By maidhood, honour, truth and every thing,
I love thee so, that, maugre all thy pride,
Nor wit nor reason can my passion hide.
[Do not extort thy reasons from this clause,
For that I woo, thou therefore hast no cause,
But rather reason thus with reason fetter,
Love sought is good, but giv'n unsought is better.]

VIOLA   **By innocence I swear, and by my youth**
220 **I have one heart, one bosom and one truth,**
And that no woman has. Nor never none
Shall mistress be of it, save I alone.
And so adieu, good madam. Never more
Will I my master's tears to you deplore.

OLIVIA   **Yet come again ... for thou perhaps mayst move**
That heart which now abhors, to like his love.   *(Exeunt)*

Scene 2   *[A room in Olivia's house.]*
               Enter SIR TOBY, SIR ANDREW and FABIAN.

ANDREW   **No, faith, I'll not stay a jot longer.**

SIR TOBY   **Thy reason, dear venom, give thy reason.**

FABIAN   **You must needs yield your reason, Sir Andrew.**

10 ANDREW   **Marry, I saw your niece do more favours to the**
Count's serving-man than ever she bestowed upon me. I saw't in
the orchard.

SIR TOBY   **Did she see thee the while, old boy? Tell me that.**

ANDREW   **As plain as I see you now.**

FABIAN   **This was a great argument of love in her toward you.**

20 ANDREW   **'S light, will you make an ass o' me?**

[FABIAN   I will prove it legitimate, sir, upon the oaths of judgment and reason.

SIR TOBY   And they have been grand-jurymen since before Noah was a sailor.]

FABIAN   She did show favour to the youth in your sight only to exasperate you, to awake your dormouse valour, to put fire in your heart and brimstone in your liver. You should then have accosted her, and with some excellent jests, fire-new from the mint, you should have banged the youth into dumbness. This was looked for at your hand, and this was balked. The double gilt of this opportunity you let time wash off, and you are now sailed into the north of my lady's opinion. Where you will hang like an icicle on a Dutchman's beard, unless you do redeem it by some laudable attempt either of valour or policy.

ANDREW   An't be any way, it must be with valour, for policy I hate. [I had as lief be a Brownist as a politician.]

SIR TOBY   Why then, build me thy fortunes upon the basis of valour. Challenge me the Count's youth to fight with him. Hurt him in eleven places. My niece shall take note of it, and assure thyself, there is no love-broker in the world can more prevail in man's commendation with woman than report of valour.

FABIAN   There is no way but this, Sir Andrew.

ANDREW   Will either of you bear me a challenge to him?

SIR TOBY   Go, write it in a martial hand. [Be curst and brief -- it is no matter how witty, so it be eloquent and full of invention.] **Taunt him with the licence of ink.** [If thou thou'st him some thrice, it shall not be amiss; and as many lies as will lie in thy sheet of paper, although the sheet were big enough for the bed of Ware in England, set 'em down. Go, about it. Let there be gall enough in thy ink, though thou write with a goose-pen, no matter.] **About it!**

ANDREW   Where shall I find you?

SIR TOBY   We'll call thee at the *cubiculo.* Go.

Exit SIR ANDREW.

[FABIAN   This is a dear manikin to you, Sir Toby.

SIR TOBY   I have been dear to him, lad, some two thousand strong or so.]

FABIAN   We shall have a rare letter from him. But you'll not deliver't?

SIR TOBY   Never trust me then. And by all means stir on the youth to an answer. I think oxen and wainropes cannot hale them together. For Andrew, if he were opened, and you find so much blood in his liver as will clog the foot of a flea, I'll eat the rest of the anatomy.

FABIAN   And his opposite, the youth, bears in his visage no great presage of cruelty.

Enter MARIA.

[SIR TOBY   Look, where the youngest wren of nine comes.]

MARIA   If you desire the spleen, and will laugh yourself into stitches, follow me. Yond gull Malvolio is [turned heathen, a very *renegado.*

42

For there is no Christian, that means to be saved by believing rightly, can ev‹
such impossible passages of grossness. He's] **in yellow stockings.**

SIR TOBY   And cross-gartered?

90   **MARIA   Most villainously;** [like a pedant that keeps a school in the church.
I have dogged him like his murderer;] **he does obey every point of the letter
that I dropped to betray him.   He does smile his face into more
lines than is in the new map with the augmentation of the Indies.**
[You have not seen such a thing as 'tis. I can hardly forbear hurling things at him.] **I
know my lady will strike him. If she do, he'll smile and take't for a
great favour.**

SIR TOBY   Come, bring us, bring us where he is.   *(Exeunt)*

Scene 3   *[A street.]*
                 Enter SEBASTIAN and ANTONIO.

**SEBASTIAN   I would not by my will have troubled you.
But, since you make your pleasure of your pains,
I will no further chide you.**

ANTONIO   I could not stay behind [you. My desire,
More sharp than filèd steel, did spur me forth.
10   And not all love to see you (though so much
As might have drawn one to a longer voyage)
But jealousy what might befall your travel,
Being skilless in these parts -- which to a stranger,
Unguided and unfriended, often prove
Rough and unhospitable. My willing love,
The rather by these arguments of fear,
Set forth in your pursuit.]

**SEBASTIAN   My kind Antonio,
20   I can no other answer make but thanks,**
[And thanks -- and ever oft good turns
Are shuffled off with such uncurrent pay --]
**But were my worth as is my conscience firm,
You should find better dealing. -- What's to do?
Shall we go see the relics of this town?**

ANTONIO   Tomorrow, sir. Best first go see your lodging.

**SEBASTIAN   I am not weary, and 'tis long to night.
30   I pray you, let us satisfy our eyes
With the memorials and the things of fame
That do renown this city.**

**ANTONIO   Would you'd pardon me ...
I do not without danger walk these streets.
Once, in a sea-fight, 'gainst the Count his galleys
I did some service ...** [of such note indeed,
That were I ta'en here it would scarce be answered.

40   SEBASTIAN   Belike you slew great number of his people?

43

NIO   The offence is not of such a bloody nature;
: the quality of the time and quarrel
: well have given us bloody argument.
ght have since been answered in repaying
we took from them; which, for traffic's sake,
of our city did.] **Only myself stood out.**
For which, if I be lapsèd in this place,
I shall pay dear.

50

SEBASTIAN   **Do not then walk too open.**

ANTONIO   **It doth not fit me. Hold, sir, here's my purse.**
In the south suburbs, at the Elephant,
Is best to lodge. I will bespeak our diet,
Whiles you beguile the time and feed your knowledge
With viewing of the town. There shall you have me.

60

[SEBASTIAN   Why I your purse?

ANTONIO   Haply your eye shall light upon some toy
You have desire to purchase. And your store,
I think, is not for idle markets, sir.]

SEBASTIAN I'll be your purse-bearer and leave you
For an hour.

ANTONIO   To the Elephant.

70   **SEBASTIAN**   **I do remember.**   *(Exeunt)*

Scene 4   *[Olivia's garden.]*
              Enter OLIVIA and MARIA.

OLIVIA   I have sent after him. He says he'll come.
How shall I feast him, what bestow of him?
For youth is bought more oft than begged or borrowed.
I speak too loud. Where is Malvolio?
[He is sad and civil, and suits well for a servant
With my fortunes. Where is Malvolio?]

10

MARIA   **He's coming, madam, but in very strange manner. He**
is, sure, possessed, madam.

OLIVIA   Why, what's the matter? Does he rave?

MARIA   **No, madam, he does nothing but smile. Your ladyship**
were best to have some guard about you, if he come, for, sure, the
man is tainted in's wits.

20   **OLIVIA   Go call him hither. – I am as mad as he,**
If sad and merry madness equal be.
      (Enter MALVOLIO) **How now, Malvolio?**

MALVOLIO Sweet lady, ho, ho!

OLIVIA   Smilest thou? I sent for thee upon a sad occasion.

MALVOLIO Sad, lady? I could be sad. This does make some

44

30 obstruction in the blood, this cross-gartering, but what of that? If
it please the eye of one, it is with me as the very true sonnet is:
'Please one, and please all.'

OLIVIA   Why, how dost thou, man? What is the matter with
thee?

MALVOLIO   Not black in my mind, though yellow in my legs ... [It
did come to his hands, and] commands shall be executed. I think we do
know the sweet Roman hand!

40 OLIVIA   Wilt thou go to bed, Malvolio?

MALVOLIO   To bed? Ay, sweetheart, and I'll come to thee.

OLIVIA   God comfort thee! [Why dost thou smile so and kiss thy hand so
oft?

MARIA   How do you, Malvolio?

MALVOLIO   At your request! Yes, nightingales answer daws.]

50 MARIA   Why appear you with this ridiculous boldness before
my lady?

MALVOLIO   "Be not afraid of greatness" – 'twas well writ.

OLIVIA   What meanest thou by that, Malvolio?

MALVOLIO   "Some are born great" –

60 OLIVIA   Ha!

MALVOLIO   "Some achieve greatness" –

OLIVIA   What sayest thou?

MALVOLIO   "And some have greatness thrust upon them."

OLIVIA   Heaven restore thee!

70 MALVOLIO   "Remember who commended thy yellow stockings" –

[OLIVIA   Thy yellow stockings!]

MALVOLIO   "And wished to see thee cross-gartered."

[OLIVIA   Cross-gartered!]

MALVOLIO   "Go to thou art made, if thou desirest to be so" –

80 [OLIVIA   Am I made?]

MALVOLIO   "If not, let me see thee a servant still."

OLIVIA   Why, this is very midsummer madness.

    Enter SERVANT.

SERVANT   Madam, the young gentleman of the Count Orsino's is
returned. I could hardly entreat him back. He attends your
90 ladyship's pleasure.

OLIVIA   I'll come to him. *(Exit SERVANT)* Good Maria, let this

fellow be looked to. Where's my cousin Toby? Let some of my people have a special care of him. I would not have him miscarry for the half of my dowry.

Exit OLIVIA [then MARIA].

100 **MALVOLIO** [O, ho, do you come near me now?] **No worse man than Sir Toby to look to me! This concurs directly with the letter. She sends him on purpose, that I may appear stubborn to him, for she incites me to that in the letter:** ['Cast thy humble slough,' says she.] **'Be opposite with a kinsman, surly with servants'** – ['let thy tongue tang with arguments of state, put thyself into the trick of singularity;' and consequently sets down the manner how: as a sad face, a reverend carriage, a slow tongue, in the habit of some sir of note,] **and so forth.** [I have limed her; but it is Jove's doing, and Jove make me thankful!] **And when she went away now, "Let this fellow be looked to ..." "Fellow" not Malvolio, nor after my degree, but "fellow". Why, everything adheres together, that no dram of a scruple, no**
110 **scruple of a scruple, no obstacle**[, no incredulous or unsafe circumstance -- What can be said? Nothing that can be] **can come between me and the full prospect of my hopes. Well, Jove, not I, is the doer of this, and he is to be thanked.**

Enter MARIA, with SIR TOBY and FABIAN.

SIR TOBY Which way is he, in the name of sanctity? If all the devils of hell [be drawn in little, and Legion himself] **possessed him, yet I'll speak to him.**
120

FABIAN Here he is, here he is. – How is't with you, sir?

[SIR TOBY How is't with you, man?]

MALVOLIO Go off, I discard you. Let me enjoy my private. Go off.

MARIA Lo, how hollow the fiend speaks within him! Did not I tell you? Sir Toby, my lady prays you to have a care of him.

130 **MALVOLIO Aha, does she so?**

SIR TOBY Go to, go to, peace, peace. We must deal gently with him. Let me alone. How do you, Malvolio? How is't with you? What, man, defy the devil? Consider, he's an enemy to mankind.

MALVOLIO Do you know what you say?

MARIA La, [you, an] **you speak ill of the devil, how he takes it at heart! Pray God, he be not bewitched!**
140

[FABIAN Carry his water to the wise woman.

MARIA Marry, and it shall be done tomorrow morning, if I live. My lady would not lose him for more than I'll say.]

MALVOLIO How now, mistress!

MARIA O Lord.

150 **SIR TOBY Prithee, hold thy peace. This is not the way. Do you not see you move him? Let me alone with him.**

FABIAN   No way but gentleness. Gently, gently. The fiend is rough, and will not be roughly used.

SIR TOBY   Why, how now, my bawcock! How dost thou, chuck?

MALVOLIO   Sir!

160   [SIR TOBY   Ay, Biddy, come with me. What, man, 'tis not for gravity to play at cherry-pit with Satan. Hang him, foul collier!]

MARIA   Get him to say his prayers, good Sir Toby, get him to pray.

MALVOLIO   My prayers, minx!

MARIA   No, I warrant you, he will not hear of godliness.

170   **MALVOLIO**   Go, hang yourselves all! You are idle shallow things. I am not of your element. You shall know more hereafter.   *(Exit)*

SIR TOBY   Is't possible?

FABIAN   If this were played upon a stage now, I could condemn it as an improbable fiction.

[SIR TOBY   His very genius hath taken the infection of the device, man.

180   MARIA   Nay, pursue him now, lest the device take air and taint.]

FABIAN   Why, we shall make him mad indeed.

[MARIA   The house will be the quieter.]

SIR TOBY   Come, we'll have him in a dark room and bound. My niece is already in the belief that he's mad. We may carry it thus – for our pleasure and his penance – till our very pastime, tired out of breath, prompt us to have mercy on him. [At which time we will bring
190   the device to the bar and crown thee for a finder of madmen.] **But see, but see ...**

Enter SIR ANDREW.

FABIAN   More matter for a May morning.

ANDREW   Here's the challenge. Read it. I warrant there's vinegar and pepper in't.

FABIAN   Is't so saucy?
200

ANDREW   Ay, is't, I warrant him. Do but read.

SIR TOBY   Give me. *(Reads)* 'Youth, whatsoever thou art, thou art but a scurvy fellow.'

FABIAN   Good, and valiant.

[SIR TOBY   *(Reads)* 'Wonder not, nor admire not in thy mind, why I do call thee so, for I will show thee no reason for't.'
210

FABIAN   A good note that keeps you from the blow of the law.]

SIR TOBY   *(Reads)* 'Thou comest to the lady Olivia, and in my sight she uses thee kindly. But thou liest in thy throat. That is not the matter I challenge thee for.'

[FABIAN   Very brief, and to exceeding good sense *(pause)* -less.]

SIR TOBY   *(Reads)* 'I will waylay thee going home, where if it
220   **be thy chance to kill me' –**

FABIAN   Good.

SIR TOBY   *(Reads)* 'Thou killest me like a rogue and a villain.'

[FABIAN   Still you keep o' the windy side of the law. Good.]

SIR TOBY   *(Reads)* 'Fare thee well, and God have mercy upon one
of our souls. He may have mercy upon mine, but my hope is better,
230   **and so look to thyself. Thy friend, as thou usest him, and thy**
sworn enemy. – *Andrew Aguecheek.'*
– If this letter move him not, his legs cannot. I'll give it him.

MARIA   You may have very fit occasion for it. He is now in
some commerce with my lady, and will by and by depart.

SIR TOBY   Go, Sir Andrew. Scout me for him at the corner of the
orchard like a bum-bailiff. So soon as ever thou seest him, draw.
And, as thou drawest, swear horrible. For it comes to pass oft that
240   **a terrible oath, with a swaggering accent sharply twanged off,**
gives manhood more approbation than ever proof itself would
have earned him. Away!

ANDREW   Nay, let me alone for swearing.   *(Exit)*

SIR TOBY   Now will not I deliver his letter, for the behaviour of
the young gentleman gives him out to be of good capacity and
breeding. [His employment between his lord and my niece confirms no less.]
Therefore this letter, being so excellently ignorant, will breed no
250   **terror in the youth. He will find it comes from a clodpole. But, sir,**
I will deliver his challenge by word of mouth, set upon Aguecheek
a notable report of valour, and [drive the gentleman -- as I know his youth will
aptly receive it -- into a most hideous opinion of his rage, skill, fury and impetuosity;]
this will so fright them both that they will kill one another by the
look – [like cockatrices.]

Enter OLIVIA, with VIOLA.

FABIAN   Here he comes with your niece. Give them way till he
260   **take leave, and presently after him.**

SIR TOBY   I will meditate the while upon some horrid message
for a challenge.

Exeunt SIR TOBY, FABIAN and MARIA.

OLIVIA   I have said too much unto a heart of stone ...
[And laid mine honour too unchary out.
There's something in me that reproves my fault;
270   But such a headstrong potent fault it is,
That it but mocks reproof.]

VIOLA   With the same 'haviour
That your passion bears goes on my master's griefs.

48

OLIVIA   Here, wear this jewel for me. 'Tis my picture.
[Refuse it not, it hath no tongue to vex you.
And I beseech you come again tomorrow.]
What shall you ask of me that I'll deny,
280   **That honour saved may upon asking give?**

VIOLA   Nothing but this: your true love for my master.

OLIVIA   How with mine honour may I give him that
Which I have given to you?

VIOLA   I will acquit you.

OLIVIA   Well, come again tomorrow. Fare thee well.
290   A fiend like thee might bear my soul to hell.

Exit. Enter SIR TOBY and FABIAN.

SIR TOBY   Gentleman, God save thee.

VIOLA   And you, sir.

SIR TOBY   That defence thou hast, betake thee to't. Of what
nature the wrongs are thou hast done him, I know not; but thy
300   intercepter, full of despite, bloody as the hunter, attends thee at
the orchard-end; [dismount thy tuck, be yare in thy preparation, for thy assailant is]
quick, skilful and deadly.

VIOLA   You mistake, sir. I am sure no man hath any quarrel
to me. My remembrance is very free and clear from any image of
offence done to any man.

SIR TOBY   You'll find it otherwise, I assure you. Therefore, if
you hold your life at any price, betake you to your guard. For your
310   opposite hath in him what youth, strength, skill and wrath can
furnish man withal.

VIOLA   I pray you, sir, what is he?

SIR TOBY   He is knight; [dubbed with unhatched rapier and on carpet
consideration;] **but he is a devil in private brawl. Souls and bodies
hath he divorced three.** [And his incensement at this moment is so implacable,
that satisfaction can be none but by pangs of death and sepulchre. Hob, nob, is his word
– give it or take it.]
320

VIOLA   I will return again into the house and desire some
conduct of the lady. I am no fighter. I have heard of some kind of
men that put quarrels purposely on others, to taste their valour.
Belike this is a man of that quirk.

SIR TOBY   Sir, no, his indignation derives itself out of a very
competent injury. Therefore, get you on and give him his desire.
Back you shall not to the house, unless you undertake that with
me which with as much safety you might answer him. [Therefore on,
330   or strip your sword stark naked, for meddle you must, that's certain, or forswear to wear
iron about you.]

VIOLA   This is as uncivil as strange. I beseech you, do me this
courteous office, as to know of the knight what my offence to him

is. It is something of my negligence, nothing of my purpose.

SIR TOBY   I will do so.   Signior Fabian, stay you by this gentleman till my return.   *(Exit)*

340   **VIOLA**   Pray you, sir, do you know of this matter?

FABIAN   I know the knight is incensed against you, [even to a mortal arbitrement,] **but nothing of the circumstance more.**

VIOLA   I beseech you, what manner of man is he?

FABIAN   [Nothing of that wonderful promise, to read him by his form, as you are like to find him in the proof of his valour.] **He is, indeed, sir, the most skilful, bloody and fatal opposite that you could possibly have found in**
350   **any part of Illyria. Will you walk towards him? I will make your peace with him if I can.**

VIOLA   **I shall be much bound to you for't. I am one that had rather go with Sir Priest than Sir Knight. I care not who knows so much of my mettle.**

Exeunt. Enter SIR TOBY, with SIR ANDREW.

SIR TOBY   **Why, man, he's a very devil. I have not seen such a**
360   **virago. I had a pass with him, rapier, scabbard and all, and he gives me the stuck in** [with such a mortal motion, that it is inevitable. And on the answer, he pays you] **as surely as your feet hit the ground they step on.** [They say he has been fencer to the Sophy.]

ANDREW   **Pox on't, I'll not meddle with him.**

SIR TOBY   **Ay, but he will not now be pacified. Fabian can scarce hold him yonder.**

370   **ANDREW**   **Plague on't, an I thought he had been valiant and so cunning in fence, I'd have seen him damned ere I'd have challenged him. Let him let the matter slip, and I'll give him my horse, grey Capilet.**

SIR TOBY   **I'll make the motion. Stand here, make a good show on't. This shall end without the perdition of souls.** *(Aside)* **Marry, I'll ride your horse as well as I ride you.** *(Enter FABIAN and VIOLA. Aside to Fabian:)* **I have his horse to take up the quarrel. I have persuaded him the youth's a devil.**
380

FABIAN   *(Aside to Sir Toby)* **He** [is as horribly conceited of him, and] **pants and looks pale, as if a bear were at his heels.**

SIR TOBY   *(To Viola)* **There's no remedy, sir. He will fight with you for his oath' sake.** [Marry, he hath better bethought him of his quarrel, and he finds that now scarce to be worth talking of.] **Therefore draw, for the supportance of his vow. He protests he will not hurt you.**

VIOLA   *(Aside)* **Pray God defend me! A little thing would make**
390   **me tell them how much I lack of a man.**

FABIAN   **Give ground if you see him furious.**

SIR TOBY   **Come, Sir Andrew, there's no remedy. The gentleman**

will, for his honour's sake, have one bout with you. [He cannot by the *duello* avoid it.] **But he has promised me, as he is a gentleman and a soldier, he will not hurt you. Come on, to't.**

400

ANDREW   Pray God, he keep his oath!

VIOLA   I do assure you, 'tis against my will.

They draw. Enter ANTONIO.

ANTONIO   Put up your sword. If this young gentleman
Have done offence, I take the fault on me.
If you offend him, I for him defy you.

410

SIR TOBY   You, sir? Why, what are you?

ANTONIO   One, sir, that for his love dares yet do more
Than you have heard him brag to you he will.

SIR TOBY   Nay, if you be an undertaker, I am for you.

They draw. Enter OFFICERS.

FABIAN   O good Sir Toby, hold! Here come the officers.

420

SIR TOBY   I'll be with you anon.

VIOLA   Pray, sir, put your sword up, if you please.

ANDREW   Marry, will I, sir. And, for that I promised you, I'll be as good as my word. He will bear you easily and reins well.

1st OFFICER   This is the man. Do thy office.

2nd OFFICER   Antonio, I arrest thee at the suit of Count Orsino.

430

ANTONIO   You do mistake me, sir.

1st OFFICER   No, sir, no jot. I know your favour well,
Though now you have no sea-cap on your head.
– Take him away. – He knows I know him well.

ANTONIO   I must obey. *(To Viola)* This comes with seeking you.
But there's no remedy. I shall answer it.
What will you do, now my necessity

440

Makes me to ask you for my purse? It grieves me
Much more for what I cannot do for you
Than what befalls myself. You stand amazed,
But be of comfort.

2nd OFFICER   Come, sir, away.

ANTONIO   I must entreat of you some of that money.

VIOLA   What money, sir?

450

For the fair kindness you have showed me here,
And part being prompted by your present trouble,
Out of my lean and low ability
I'll lend you something. My having is not much.
[I'll make division of my present with you.]
Hold, there's half my coffer.

ANTONIO   **Will you deny me now?**
Is't possible that my deserts to you
Can lack persuasion? [Do not tempt my misery,
460   Lest that it make me so unsound a man
As to upbraid you with those kindnesses
That I have done for you.]

VIOLA   **I know of none.**
Nor know I you by voice or any feature.
[I hate ingratitude more in a man
Than lying, vainness, babbling, drunkenness,
Or any taint of vice whose strong corruption
Inhabits our frail blood.
470

ANTONIO   O heavens themselves!]

2ⁿᵈ OFFICER Come, sir, I pray you, go.

[ANTONIO   Let me speak a little. This youth that you see here
I snatched one half out of the jaws of death.
Relieved him with such sanctity of love,
And to his image, which methought did promise
Most venerable worth, did I devotion.]
480

1ˢᵗ OFFICER [What's that to us?] **The time goes by. Away!**

ANTONIO   But O how vile an idol proves this god
Thou hast, Sebastian, done good feature shame.
[In nature there's no blemish but the mind.
None can be called deformed but the unkind.
Virtue is beauty, but the beauteous evil
Are empty trunks o'erflourished by the devil.]

490   **1ˢᵗ OFFICER The man grows mad. Away with him! Come, come, sir.**

ANTONIO   Lead me on.

         Exit with OFFICERS.

VIOLA   Methinks his words do from such passion fly,
That he believes himself ... So do not I ...
Prove true, imagination, O, prove true,
That I, dear brother, be now ta'en for you!
500

[SIR TOBY   Come hither, knight. Come hither, Fabian. We'll whisper o'er a couplet
or two of most sage saws.

VIOLA   He named Sebastian ... I my brother know
Yet living in my glass. Even such and so
In favour was my brother, and he went
Still in this fashion, colour, ornament,
For him I imitate... O, if it prove,
Tempests are kind and salt waves fresh in love!]   *(Exit)*
510

SIR TOBY   A very dishonest paltry boy, and more a coward than
a hare: [his dishonesty appears in leaving his friend here in necessity and denying him.
And for his cowardship] – **ask Fabian.**

FABIAN	A coward, a most devout coward, religious in i█	
ANDREW	'S lid, I'll after him again and beat him.	
SIR TOBY	Do. Cuff him soundly, but never draw thy sword.	
ANDREW	An I do not –	
FABIAN	Come, let's see the event.	
SIR TOBY	I dare lay any money 'twill be nothing yet.	*(Exeunt)*

520 (line marker beside SIR TOBY/ANDREW)

ACT FOUR
Scene 1   *[Outside Olivia's house.]*
Enter SEBASTIAN and FESTE.

FESTE   Will you make me believe that I am not sent for you?

SEBASTIAN   Go to, go to, thou art a foolish fellow. [Let me be clear of thee.]

10   **FESTE**   [Well held out, i' faith.] **No, I do not know you. Nor I am not sent to you by my lady to bid you come speak with her. Nor your name is not Master Cesario. Nor this is not my nose neither.** [Nothing that is so is so.]

SEBASTIAN   **I prithee, vent thy folly somewhere else. Thou know'st not me.**

FESTE   **"Vent my folly"! He has heard that word of some great man and now applies it to a fool. Vent my folly!** [I am afraid this 20 great lubber, the world, will prove a cockney ...] **I prithee now,** [ungird thy strangeness and] **tell me what I shall "vent" to my lady. Shall I "vent" to her that thou art coming?**

SEBASTIAN   **I prithee, foolish Greek, depart from me. There's money for thee.** [If you tarry longer, I shall give worse payment.]

FESTE   **By my troth, thou hast an open hand.** [These wise men that give fools money get themselves a good report -- after fourteen years' purchase.]

30   *Enter SIR ANDREW, SIR TOBY and FABIAN.*

ANDREW   **Now, sir, have I met you again?** *(Strikes him)* **There's for you.**

SEBASTIAN   *(Striking him)* **Why, there's for thee, and there, and there! Are all the people mad?**

SIR TOBY   **Hold, sir, or I'll throw your dagger o'er the house.**

40   **FESTE**   **This will I tell my lady straight. I would not be in some of your coats for twopence.**   *(Exit)*

SIR TOBY   **Come on, sir, hold.**

ANDREW   **Nay, let him alone. I'll go another way to work with him. I'll have an action of battery against him, if there be any law**

yria. **Though I struck him first ... yet it's no matter for that.**

TIAN **Let go thy hand.**

BY **Come, sir, I will not let you go. Come, my young
er, put up your iron.** [You are well fleshed.] **Come on.**

TIAN **I will be free from thee.** (Frees himself) **What wouldst
thou now? If thou darest tempt me further, draw thy sword.**

**SIR TOBY   What, what? Nay, then I must have an ounce or two
of this malapert blood from you.**

60   *Enter OLIVIA.*

OLIVIA   Hold, Toby. On thy life I charge thee, hold!

SIR TOBY   Madam!

**OLIVIA   Will it be ever thus? Ungracious wretch,
Fit for the mountains and the barbarous caves,
Where manners ne'er were preached! Out of my sight!
Be not offended, dear Cesario.**

70   **– Rudesby, be gone!**   (Exeunt SIR TOBY, SIR ANDREW and FABIAN)
**I prithee, gentle friend,
Let thy fair wisdom, not thy passion, sway
In this uncivil and thou unjust extent
Against thy peace. Go with me to my house,
And hear thou there how many fruitless pranks
This ruffian hath botched up, that thou thereby
Mayst smile at this. Thou shalt not choose but go.**
[Do not deny. Beshrew his soul for me,
He started one poor heart of mine in thee.]

80

SEBASTIAN [What relish is in this? How runs the stream?]
Or I am mad, or else this is a dream.
[Let fancy still my sense in Lethe steep.]
If it be thus to dream, still let me sleep!

OLIVIA   Nay, come, I prithee. Would thou'ldst be ruled by me?

SEBASTIAN   Madam, I will.

90   **OLIVIA   O, say so, and so be.**   (Exeunt)

Scene 2   *[A room in Olivia's house.]*
Enter MARIA and FESTE.

**MARIA   Nay, I prithee, put on this gown and this beard. Make
him believe thou art Sir Topas the curate. Do it quickly. I'll call
Sir Toby the whilst.**   (Exit)

**FESTE   Well, I'll put it on, and I will dissemble myself in't ...
and I would I were the first that ever dissembled in such a gown.** [I
10   am not tall enough to become the function well, nor lean enough to be thought a good
student, but to be said an honest man and a good housekeeper goes as fairly as to say a
careful man and a great scholar.] **-- The competitors enter.**

Enter SIR TOBY [and MARIA].

SIR TOBY   Jove bless thee, master Parson.

FESTE   *Bonos dies*, **Sir Toby.**[For, as the old hermit of Prague, that never saw pen and ink, very wittily said to a niece of King Gorboduc: 'That that is, is.' So I, being Master Parson, am Master Parson. For, what is 'that' but 'that,' and 'is' but 'is'?]

20

SIR TOBY   To him, Sir Topas.

FESTE   What, ho, I say! Peace in this prison!

SIR TOBY   The knave counterfeits well. A good knave.

MALVOLIO   *(Within)* Who calls there?

30 **FESTE**   Sir Topas the curate, who comes to visit Malvolio the lunatic.

MALVOLIO   Sir Topas, Sir Topas, good Sir Topas, go to my lady.

FESTE   Out, hyperbolical fiend! How vexest thou this man! Talkest thou nothing but of ladies?

SIR TOBY   Well said, Master Parson.

40 **MALVOLIO**   Sir Topas, never was man thus wronged. Good Sir Topas, do not think I am mad. They have laid me here in hideous darkness.

FESTE   Fie, thou dishonest Satan! [I call thee by the most modest terms, for I am one of those gentle ones that will use the devil himself with courtesy.] Sayest thou that house is dark?

MALVOLIO   As hell, Sir Topas.

50 **FESTE**   Why it hath bay windows transparent as barricadoes! [And the clearstores toward the south-north are as lustrous as ebony ... and yet complainest thou of obstruction?]

MALVOLIO   I am not mad, Sir Topas. I say to you, this house is dark.

FESTE   Madman, thou errest. [I say, there is no darkness but ignorance; in which thou art more puzzled than the Egyptians in their fog.]

60 **MALVOLIO**   I say, this house is as dark as ignorance, [though ignorance were as dark as hell.] and I say, there was never man thus abused. I am no more mad than you are. [Make the trial of it in any constant question.

FESTE   What is the opinion of Pythagoras concerning wild fowl?

MALVOLIO   That the soul of our grandam might haply inhabit a bird.

FESTE   What thinkest thou of his opinion?

70 MALVOLIO   I think nobly of the soul, and no way approve his opinion.

FESTE   Fare thee well. Remain thou still in darkness. Thou shalt hold the opinion of Pythagoras ere I will allow of thy wits, and fear to kill a woodcock, lest thou dispossess the soul of thy grandam. Fare thee well.

MALVOLIO   Sir Topas, Sir Topas!

SIR TOBY   My most exquisite Sir Topas!

80   FESTE   Nay, I am for all waters!]

MARIA   **Thou mightst have done this without thy beard and gown. He sees thee not.**

SIR TOBY   **To him in thine own voice, and bring me word how thou findest him. I would we were well rid of this knavery. If he may be conveniently delivered, I would he were, for I am now so far in offence with my niece that I cannot pursue with any safety this sport to the upshot. – Come by and by to my chamber.**

90

Exit SIR TOBY [with MARIA].

FESTE *(Sings)*   **"Hey, Robin, jolly Robin,**
Tell me how thy lady does."

MALVOLIO   **Fool.**

FESTE   **"My lady is unkind, perdie."**

100   **MALVOLIO**   **Fool!**

FESTE   **"Alas, why is she so?"**

MALVOLIO   **Fool, I say!**

FESTE   **"She loves another." – Who calls, ha?**

MALVOLIO   **Good fool, as ever thou wilt deserve well at my hand, help me to a candle, and pen, ink and paper. As I am a gentleman, I will live to be thankful to thee for't.**

110

FESTE   **Master Malvolio?**

MALVOLIO   **Ay, good fool.**

FESTE   **Alas, sir, how fell you besides your five wits?**

MALVOLIO   **Fool, there was never a man so notoriously abused. I am as well in my wits, fool, as thou art.**

120

FESTE   [But as well?] **Then you are mad indeed, if you be no better in your wits than a fool.**

MALVOLIO   **They** [have here propertied me,] **keep me in darkness, send ministers to me, asses, and do all they can to face me out of my wits.**

FESTE   **Advise you what you say. The minister is here.** *(As Sir Topas)* **Malvolio, Malvolio, thy wits the heavens restore! Endeavour thyself to sleep, and leave thy vain bibble-babble.**

130

MALVOLIO   **Sir Topas!**

FESTE   **Maintain no words with him, good fellow.** *(As himself)* **Who, I, sir? Not I, sir. God be wi' you, good Sir Topas.** *(As Sir Topas)* **Merry, amen.** *(As himself)* **I will, sir, I will.**

MALVOLIO   **Fool, fool, fool, I say!**

140   **FESTE**   **Alas, sir, be patient.** [What say you sir? I am shent for speaki͟ you.]

MALVOLIO   **Good fool, help me to some light and some paper.** [I tell thee, I am as well in my wits as any man in Illyria.

FESTE   Well-a-day that you were, sir

MALVOLIO   [By this hand, I am. Good fool, some ink, paper and light.] **And convey what I will set down to my lady. It shall advantage thee** 150   **more than ever the bearing of letter did.**

FESTE   **I will help you to't. But tell me true, are you not mad indeed? Or do you but counterfeit?**

MALVOLIO   **Believe me, I am not. I tell thee true.**

FESTE   **Nay, I'll ne'er believe a madman till I see his brains. I will fetch you light and paper and ink.**

160   **MALVOLIO**   **Fool, I'll requite it in the highest degree. I prithee, be gone.**

FESTE   *(Sings)*   **I am gone, sir.**
              [And anon, sir,
                  I'll be with you again,
              In a trice,
              Like to the old Vice,
                  Your need to sustain.
              Who, with dagger of lath,
170   In his rage and his wrath,
                  Cries 'Aha!' to the devil.
              Like a mad lad,
              'Pare thy nails, dad.'
                  Adieu, goodman devil.   *(Exit)*

Scene 3   *[Olivia's garden.]*
             Enter SEBASTIAN.

SEBASTIAN   **This is the air, that is the glorious sun.**
  This pearl she gave me, I do feel't and see't;
  And though 'tis wonder that enwraps me thus,
  Yet 'tis not madness. — Where's Antonio then?
  I could not find him at the Elephant,
  Yet there he was ... and there I found this credit:
10   **That he did range the town to seek me out.**
  [His counsel now might do me golden service;
  For though my soul disputes well with my sense
  That this may be some error but no madness,
  Yet doth this accident and flood of fortune
  So far exceed all instance, all discourse,
  That I am ready to distrust mine eyes,
  And wrangle with my reason that persuades me
  To any other trust but that I am mad --

se the lady's mad. Yet if 'twere so,
ould not sway her house, command her followers,
and give back affairs and their dispatch
such a smooth, discreet and stable bearing
erceive she does. There's something in't
s deceivable.] **But here the lady comes.**

Enter OLIVIA and PRIEST.

OLIVIA   **Blame not this haste of mine. If you mean well,**
Now go with me and with this holy man
30   **Into the chantry by. There, before him,**
And underneath that consecrated roof,
Plight me the full assurance of your faith,
That my most jealous and too doubtful soul
May live at peace. He shall conceal it
Whiles you are willing it shall come to note,
What time we will our celebration keep
According to my birth. What do you say?

SEBASTIAN **I'll follow this good man, and go with you**
40   **And, having sworn truth, ever will be true.**

OLIVIA   **Then lead the way, good father, and heavens so shine**
That they may fairly note this act of mine.   *(Exeunt)*

ACT FIVE
Scene 1   *[Outside Olivia's house.]*
Enter FESTE and FABIAN.

FABIAN   **Now, as thou lovest me, let me see his letter.**

FESTE   **Good Master Fabian, grant me another request.**

FABIAN   **Anything.**
10

FESTE   **Do not desire to see this letter.**

FABIAN   **This is to give a dog, and in recompense desire my dog**
again.

Enter DUKE ORSINO, VIOLA, CURIO [and LORDS].

ORSINO   **Belong you to the Lady Olivia, friends?**

20   **FESTE**   **Ay, sir, we are some of her trappings.**

ORSINO   **I know thee well. How dost thou, my good fellow?**

FESTE   **Truly, sir, the better for my foes and the worse for my**
friends.

ORSINO   **Just the contrary. The better for thy friends.**

FESTE   **No, sir, the worse.**
30

ORSINO   How can that be?

FESTE   Marry, sir, they praise me and make an ass of me. Now my foes tell me plainly I am an ass ... so that by my foes, sir, I profit in the knowledge of myself, and by my friends, I am abused. [So that, conclusions to be as kisses, if your four negatives make your two affirmatives why then, the worse for my friends and the better for my foes.]

40

ORSINO   Why, this is excellent.

FESTE   By my troth, sir, no, though it please you to be one of my friends.

ORSINO   Thou shalt not be the worse for me. There's gold.

FESTE   But that it would be double-dealing, sir ... I would you could make it another.

50

[ORSINO   O, you give me ill counsel.

FESTE   Put your grace in your pocket, sir, for this once, and let your flesh and blood obey it.

ORSINO   Well, I will be so much a sinner to be a double-dealer -- there's another.

FESTE   *Primo, secundo, tertio,* is a good play, and the old saying is, the third pays for all. The triplex, sir, is a good tripping measure, or the bells of Saint Bennet, sir, may put you in mind: 'One, two, three'?]

60

ORSINO   You can fool no more money out of me at this throw. If you will let your lady know I am here to speak with her, and bring her along with you, it may awake my bounty further.

FESTE   Marry, sir, [lullaby to your bounty till I come again. I go, sir, but I would not have you to think that my desire of having is the sin of covetousness. But,] **as you say, sir, let your bounty take a nap, I will awake it anon.** *(Exit)*

VIOLA   Here comes the man, sir, that did rescue me.

70

Enter ANTONIO and OFFICERS.

ORSINO   That face of his I do remember well. Yet, when I saw it last, it was besmeared As black as Vulcan in the smoke of war.
[A bawbling vessel was he captain of, For shallow draught and bulk unprizable; With which such scatheful grapple did he make With the most noble bottom of our fleet, That very envy and the tongue of loss

80

Cried fame and honour on him. -- What's the matter?]

1st OFFICER   Orsino, this is that Antonio That took the Phoenix and her fraught from Candy.
[And this is he that did the 'Tiger' board, When your young nephew Titus lost his leg.]
Here in the streets, desperate of shame and state, In private brabble did we apprehend him.

VIOLA   He did me kindness, sir, drew on my side,

90   **But in conclusion put strange speech upon me.**
    I know not what 'twas but distraction.

ORSINO   **Notable pirate, thou salt-water thief,**
What foolish boldness brought thee to their mercies,
Whom thou, in terms so bloody and so dear,
Hast made thine enemies?

ANTONIO   **Orsino, noble sir,**
[Be pleased that I shake off these names you give me.]
100   **Antonio never yet was thief or pirate,**
    Though I confess, on base and ground enough,
    Orsino's enemy. A witchcraft drew me hither.
    That most ingrateful boy there by your side,
    From the rude sea's enraged and foamy mouth
    Did I redeem. A wreck past hope he was.
    [His life I gave him and did thereto add
    My love without retention or restraint,
    All his in dedication.] **For his sake**
    Did I expose myself, [pure for his love,]
110   **Into the danger of this adverse town;**
    Drew to defend him when he was beset,
    Where being apprehended, his false cunning
    [--Not meaning to partake with me in danger --
    Taught him to face me out of his acquaintance,
    And grew a twenty years removed thing
    While one would wink;] **denied me mine own purse,**
    Which I had recommended to his use
    Not half an hour before.

120   **VIOLA**   **How can this be?**

ORSINO   **When came he to this town?**

ANTONIO   **Today, my lord, and for three months before,**
No interim, not a minute's vacancy,
Both day and night did we keep company.

    Enter OLIVIA [and ATTENDANTS].

130   **ORSINO**   **Here comes the Countess** -- [Now heaven walks on earth.
But for thee, fellow:] **fellow, thy words are madness.**
Three months this youth hath tended upon me.
But more of that anon. Take him aside.

OLIVIA   **What would my lord, but that he may not have,**
Wherein Olivia may seem serviceable?
Cesario, you do not keep promise with me.

140   **VIOLA**   **Madam?**

ORSINO   **Gracious Olivia –**

OLIVIA   **What do you say, Cesario? – Good my lord –**

VIOLA   **My lord would speak; my duty hushes me.**

OLIVIA   **If it be aught to the old tune, my lord,**

It is as fat and fulsome to mine ear
As howling after music.

150

ORSINO   Still so cruel?

OLIVIA   Still so constant, lord.

ORSINO   What, to perverseness? You uncivil lady –
To whose ingrate and unauspicious altars
My soul the faithfull'st offerings hath breathed out
That e'er devotion tendered – what shall I do?

160   OLIVIA   Even what it please my lord, that shall become him.

ORSINO   Why should I not, had I the heart to do it,
[Like to the Egyptian thief at point of death,]
Kill what I love? – [a savage jealousy
That sometimes savours nobly.] **But hear me this:**
[Since you to non-regardance cast my faith,
And that I partly know the instrument
That screws me from my true place in your favour,]
Live you the marble-breasted tyrant still,
170   **But this your minion, whom I know you love,**
[And whom, by heaven, I swear I tender dearly,]
Him will I tear out of that cruel eye,
Where he sits crownèd in his master's spite.
Come, boy, with me. My thoughts are ripe in mischief.
I'll sacrifice the lamb that I do love,
To spite a raven's heart within a dove.

VIOLA   And I, most jocund, apt and willingly,
To do you rest, a thousand deaths would die.

180

OLIVIA   Where goes Cesario?

VIOLA   After him I love –
[More than I love these eyes, more than my life,
More, by all mores, than e'er I shall love wife.
If I do feign, you witnesses above,
Punish my life for tainting of my love!]

190   OLIVIA   Ay me, detested! How am I beguiled!

VIOLA   Who does beguile you? Who does do you wrong?

OLIVIA   Hast thou forgot thyself? Is it so long?
Call forth the holy father.

ORSINO   *(To Viola)* **Come, away!**

OLIVIA   Whither, my lord? Cesario, husband, stay.

200   ORSINO   Husband?

OLIVIA   Ay, husband. Can he that deny?

ORSINO   Her husband, sirrah?

VIOLA   No, my lord, not I.

OLIVIA   [Alas, it is the baseness of thy fear
That makes thee strangle thy propriety.]
210 **Fear not, Cesario. Take thy fortunes up.
Be that thou know'st thou art, and then thou art
As great as that thou fear'st.** *(Enter PRIEST)* **O, welcome, father!
Father, I charge thee, by thy reverence,
Here to unfold** [-- though lately we intended
To keep in darkness what occasion now
Reveals before 'tis ripe --] **what thou dost know
Hath newly passed between this youth and me.**

PRIEST   **A contract of eternal bond of love,**
220 [Confirmed by mutual joinder of your hands,
Attested by the holy close of lips,
Strengthened by interchangement of your rings,
And all the ceremony of this compact]
**Sealed in my function, by my testimony --
Since when, my watch hath told me, toward my grave
I have travelled but two hours.**

ORSINO   **O thou dissembling cub,** [what wilt thou be
When time hath sowed a grizzle on thy case?
230 Or will not else thy craft so quickly grow,
That thine own trip shall be thine overthrow?
Farewell and take her, but] **direct thy feet
Where thou and I henceforth may never meet.**

VIOLA   **My lord, I do protest --**

OLIVIA   **O, do not swear!
Hold little faith, though thou hast too much fear.**

240   *Enter SIR ANDREW.*

ANDREW   **For the love of God, a surgeon! Send one presently to
Sir Toby!**

OLIVIA   **What's the matter?**

ANDREW   **He has broke my head across and has given Sir Toby
a bloody coxcomb too. For the love of God, your help! I had rather
than forty pound I were at home.**
250
OLIVIA   **Who has done this, Sir Andrew?**

ANDREW   **The Count's gentleman, one Cesario. We took him for
a coward, but he's the very devil incardinate.**

ORSINO   **My gentleman, Cesario?**

ANDREW   **'Od's lifelings, here he is!** [You broke my head for nothing ...
and that that I did, I was set on to do't by Sir Toby.]
260
VIOLA   **Why do you speak to me? I never hurt you.
You drew your sword upon me without cause.
But I bespoke you fair, and hurt you not.**

ANDREW   **If a bloody coxcomb be a hurt, you have hurt me. I
think you set nothing by a bloody coxcomb.** *(Enter SIR TOBY and*

FESTE) **Here comes Sir Toby, halting. You shall hear more.** [But if he had not been in drink, he would have tickled you othergates than he did.]

270 **ORSINO** **How now, gentleman, how is't with you?**

SIR TOBY **That's all one. He's hurt me, and there's the end on't. - - Sot, didst see Dick surgeon, sot?**

FESTE **Oh, he's drunk, Sir Toby, an hour agone.** [His eyes were set at eight i' the morning.]

SIR TOBY [Then he's a rogue, and a passy measures pavin.] **I hate a drunken**
280 **rogue.**

OLIVIA **Away with him! Who hath made this havoc with them?**

ANDREW **I'll help you, Sir Toby ...** [because we'll be dressed together.]

SIR TOBY **Will you help? An ass-head and a coxcomb and a knave, a thin-faced knave, a gull?**

OLIVIA **Get him to bed, and let his hurt be looked to.**

290 *Exeunt FESTE, FABIAN, SIR TOBY and SIR ANDREW. Enter SEBASTIAN.* + MARIA

SEBASTIAN **I am sorry, madam, I have hurt your kinsman.**
[But, had it been the brother of my blood,
I must have done no less with wit and safety.]
**You throw a strange regard upon me, and by that
I do perceive it hath offended you.
Pardon me, sweet one, even for the vows
We made each other but so late ago.**
300

ORSINO **One face, one voice, one habit, and two persons ...
A natural perspective, that is and is not!**

SEBASTIAN **Antonio, O my dear Antonio!
How have the hours racked and tortured me,
Since I have lost thee!**

ANTONIO **Sebastian are you?**

310 **SEBASTIAN** **Fear'st thou that, Antonio?**

ANTONIO **How have you made division of yourself?
An apple, cleft in two, is not more twin
Than these two creatures ... Which is Sebastian?**

OLIVIA **Most wonderful!**

SEBASTIAN **Do I stand there? I never had a brother.
Nor can there be that deity in my nature
320 Of here and everywhere. I had a sister,
Whom the blind waves and surges have devoured.
- Of charity, what kin are you to me?
What countryman, what name, what parentage?**

VIOLA **Of Messaline. Sebastian was my father.
Such a Sebastian was my brother too,**

So went he suited to his watery tomb.
If spirits can assume both form and suit
You come to fright us.

330

SEBASTIAN   A spirit I am indeed,
But am in that dimension grossly clad
Which from the womb I did participate.
Were you a woman, as the rest goes even,
I should my tears let fall upon your cheek,
And say 'Thrice-welcome, drownèd Viola!'

VIOLA   My father had a mole upon his brow.

340 **SEBASTIAN** And so had mine.

VIOLA   And died that day when Viola from her birth
Had numbered thirteen years.

[SEBASTIAN   O, that record is lively in my soul!
He finished indeed his mortal act
That day that made my sister thirteen years.

VIOLA   If nothing lets to make us happy both
350   But this my masculine usurped attire,
Do not embrace me till each circumstance
Of place, time, fortune, do cohere and jump
That I am Viola; which to confirm,
I'll bring you to a captain in this town,
Where lie my maiden weeds, by whose gentle help
I was preserved to serve this noble count.
All the occurrence of my fortune since
Hath been between this lady and this lord.]

360 **SEBASTIAN** *(To Olivia)* **So comes it, lady, you have been mistook.**
[But nature to her bias drew in that.]
**You would have been contracted to a maid.
Nor are you therein, by my life, deceived.
You are betrothed both to a maid and man.**

ORSINO   Be not amazed. Right noble is his blood.
If this be so, as yet the glass seems true,
I shall have share in this most happy wrack.
(To Viola) Boy, thou hast said to me a thousand times
370   Thou never shouldst love woman like to me.

VIOLA   And all those sayings will I overswear.
[And those swearings keep as true in soul
As doth that orbèd continent the fire
That severs day from night.]

ORSINO   Give me thy hand,
And let me see thee in thy woman's weeds.

380 **VIOLA**   The captain that did bring me first on shore
Hath my maid's garments. He, upon some action
Is now in durance at Malvolio's suit,
A gentleman, and follower of my lady's.

64

OLIVIA   He shall enlarge him. – Fetch Malvolio hither.
And yet, alas, now I remember me,
They say, poor gentleman, he's much distract.
(Enter FESTE with a letter, and FABIAN)
[A most extracting frenzy of mine own
390   From my remembrance clearly banished his.]
How does he, sirrah?

FESTE   Truly, madam, he holds Belzebub at the stave's end as
well as a man in his case may do.   He's here writ a letter to you.
[I should have given't you today morning, but as a madman's epistles are no gospels, so it
skills not much when they are delivered.]

OLIVIA   Open it and read it.

400   FESTE   Look then to be well edified when the fool delivers
the madman. *(Reads)* 'By the Lord, madam' –

OLIVIA   How now, art thou mad?

FESTE   No, madam, I do but read madness. [An your ladyship will
have it as it ought to be, you must allow **vox.**]

OLIVIA   Prithee, read in thy right wits.

410   FESTE   So I do, madonna, but to read his right wits is to read
thus. [Therefore perpend, my princess, and give ear.]

OLIVIA   Read it you, sirrah. *(To Fabian)*

FABIAN   *(Reads)* 'By the Lord, madam, you wrong me, and the
world shall know it. Though you have put me into darkness and
given your drunken cousin rule over me, yet have I the benefit of
my senses as well as your ladyship. I have your own letter that
induced me to the semblance I put on – with the which I doubt not
420   but to do myself much right, or you much shame. Think of me as
you please. I leave my duty a little unthought of and speak out of
my injury.   – *The madly-used Malvolio.*'

OLIVIA   Did he write this?

FESTE   Ay, madam.

ORSINO   This savours not much of distraction.

430   OLIVIA   See him delivered, Fabian. Bring him hither.
[(Exit FABIAN)]
My lord so please you, these things further thought on,
To think me as well a sister as a wife,
One day shall crown the alliance on't, so please you,
Here at my house and at my proper cost.

ORSINO   Madam, I am most apt to embrace your offer.
(To Viola) Your master quits you. And for your service done him,
So much against the mettle of your sex,
440   So far beneath your soft and tender breeding,
And since you called me master for so long,
Here is my hand. You shall from this time be
Your master's mistress.

65

OLIVIA   A sister! You are she.

Enter [FABIAN with] MALVOLIO.

450
ORSINO   Is this the madman?

OLIVIA   Ay, my lord, this same.
How now, Malvolio?

MALVOLIO   Madam, you have done me wrong,
Notorious wrong.

OLIVIA   Have I, Malvolio? No.

MALVOLIO Lady, you have. Pray you, peruse that letter.
460   You must not now deny it is your hand.
[Write from it, if you can, in hand or phrase,
Or say 'tis not your seal, nor your invention ...
You can say none of this? Well, grant it then
And tell me, in the modesty of honour,
Why you have given me such clear lights of favour,
Bade me come smiling and cross-gartered to you,
To put on yellow stockings and to frown
Upon Sir Toby and the lighter people.
And, acting this in an obedient hope,
470   Why have you suffered me to be imprisoned,
Kept in a dark house, visited by the priest,
And made the most notorious geck and gull
That e'er invention played on? Tell me why.]

OLIVIA   Alas, Malvolio, this is not my writing,
Though, I confess, much like the character.
But out of question 'tis Maria's hand.
[And now I do bethink me, it was she
First told me thou wast mad; then camest in smiling,
480   And in such forms which here were presupposed
Upon thee in the letter. -- Prithee, be content.]
This practise hath most shrewdly passed upon thee;
But when we know the grounds and authors of it,
Thou shalt be both the plaintiff and the judge
Of thine own cause.

FABIAN   Good madam, hear me speak,
[And let no quarrel nor no brawl to come
Taint the condition of this present hour,
490   Which I have wondered at. In hope it shall not,]
Most freely I confess, myself and Toby
Set this device against Malvolio here,
[Upon some stubborn and uncourteous parts
We had conceived against him. Maria writ
The letter at Sir Toby's great importance,
In recompense whereof he hath married her.
How with a sportful malice it was followed
May rather pluck on laughter than revenge,
If that the injuries be justly weighed
500   That have on both sides passed.]

66

OLIVIA   Alas, poor fool, how have they baffled thee!

FESTE   Why, "some are born great, some achieve greatness, and some have greatness thrown upon them." I was one, sir, in this interlude, one Sir Topas, sir. [But that's all one. "By the Lord, fool, I am not mad."] But do you remember "Madam, why laugh you at such a barren rascal? An you smile not, he's gagged." -- And thus the whirligig of time brings in his revenges.

510

MALVOLIO   I'll be revenged on the whole pack of you!   *(Exit)*

OLIVIA   He hath been most notoriously abused.

ORSINO   Pursue him and entreat him to a peace.
He hath not told us of the captain yet.
When that is known and golden time convents,
A solemn combination shall be made
Of our dear souls. Meantime, sweet sister,
520   We will not part from hence. -- Cesario, come ...
For so you shall be, while you are a man;
But when in other habits you are seen,
Orsino's mistress and his fancy's queen.

Exeunt all, except FESTE.

FESTE *(Sings)* When that I was and a little tiny boy --
                With hey, ho, the wind and the rain --
            A foolish thing was but a toy,
530   For the rain, it raineth every day.

            [But when I came to man's estate --
                With hey, ho, the wind and the rain --
            'Gainst knaves and thieves men shut their gate,
                For the rain, it raineth every day.]

            But when I came, alas, to wive --
                With hey, ho, the wind and the rain --
            By swaggering could I never thrive,
540   For the rain, it raineth every day.

            [But when I came unto my beds --
                With hey, ho, the wind and the rain --
            With toss-pots still had drunken heads,
                For the rain, it raineth every day.]

            A great while ago the world begun --
                With hey, ho, the wind and the rain --
            But that's all one, our play is done,
550   And we'll strive to please you every day.   *(Exit)*

Much Ado About Nothing

by William Shakespeare

LIST OF CHARACTERS

DON PEDRO	Prince of Arragon
DON JOHN	his bastard brother
CLAUDIO	a young lord of Florence
BENEDICK	a young lord of Padua
LEONATO	Governor of Messina
ANTONIO	his brother
BALTHASAR	attendant on Don Pedro
CONRADE	follower of Don John
BORACHIO	follower of Don John
FRIAR FRANCIS	
DOGBERRY	a constable
VERGES	a headborough
A SEXTON	
A BOY	

HERO	daughter to Leonato
BEATRICE	niece to Leonato
MARGARET	gentlewoman waiting on Hero
URSULA	gentlewoman waiting on Hero

LORD
MESSENGER
1st and 2nd WATCHMAN ("TheWatch")
[ATTENDANTS and MUSICIANS]

Scene: Messina

ACT ONE

Scene 1   *[Outside Leonato's house.]*
Enter LEONATO, HERO and BEATRICE with a Messenger.

LEONATO   **I learn in this letter that Don Pedro of Arragon comes this night to Messina.**

MESS.   **He is very near by this. He was not three leagues off when I left him.**

10

[LEONATO   How many gentlemen have you lost in this action?

MESSENGER   But few of any sort, and none of name.]

LEONATO   **A victory is twice itself when the achiever brings home full numbers. I find here that Don Pedro hath bestowed much honour on a young Florentine called Claudio.**

MESS.   **Much deserved on his part and equally remembered by Don Pedro. He hath borne himself beyond the promise of his age, doing, in the figure of a lamb, the feats of a lion.** [He hath indeed better bettered expectation than you must expect of me to tell you how.]

20

LEONATO   **He hath an uncle here in Messina will be very much glad of it.**

[MESSENGER   I have already delivered him letters, and there appears much joy in him -- even so much that joy could not show itself modest enough without a badge of bitterness.

30

LEONATO   Did he break out into tears?

MESSENGER   In great measure.

LEONATO   A kind overflow of kindness. There are no faces truer than those that are so washed. How much better is it to weep at joy than to joy at weeping!]

BEATRICE   **I pray you, is Signior Mountanto returned from the wars or no?**

40

MESS.   **I know none of that name, lady. There was none such in the army of any sort.**

LEONATO   **What is he that you ask for, niece?**

HERO   **My cousin means Signior Benedick of Padua.**

MESS.   **O, he's returned, and as pleasant as ever he was.**

50   **BEATRICE**   [He set up his bills here in Messina and challenged Cupid at the flight. And my uncle's fool, reading the challenge, subscribed for Cupid and challenged him at the bird-bolt.] **I pray you, how many hath he killed and eaten in these wars? But how many hath he killed? – For indeed I promised to eat all of his killing.**

LEONATO   **Faith, niece, you tax Signior Benedick too much. But he'll be meet with you, I doubt it not.**

MESS.   **He hath done good service, lady, in these wars.**

60

BEATRICE　You had musty victual, and he hath help to eat it? He [is a very valiant trencherman; he] **hath an excellent stomach.**

MESENGER　And a good soldier too, lady.

BEATRICE　And a good soldier to a lady. But what is he to a lord?

MESS.　A lord to a lord, a man to a man. Stuffed with all honourable virtues.

70

BEATRICE　It is so, indeed. He is no less than a stuffed man − but for the stuffing … well, we are all mortal.

LEONATO　You must not, sir, mistake my niece. There is a kind of merry war betwixt Signior Benedick and her. They never meet but there's a skirmish of wit between them.

BEATRICE　Alas, he gets nothing by that. In our last conflict four of his five wits went halting off, and now is the whole man governed with one. [So that if he have wit enough to keep himself warm, let him bear it for a difference between himself and his horse; for it is all the wealth that he hath left: to be known a reasonable creature.] **Who is his companion now? He hath every month a new sworn brother.**

80

[MESS.　Is't possible?]

BEATRICE　[Very easily possible.] **He wears his faith but as the fashion of his hat.** [It ever changes with the next block.]

90　**MESS.**　I see, lady, the gentleman is not in your books.

BEATRICE　No. An he were, I would burn my study. But, I pray you, who is his companion? Is there no young squarer now that will make a voyage with him to the devil?

MESS.　He is most in the company of the right noble Claudio.

BEATRICE　O Lord, he will hang upon him like a disease. [He is sooner caught than the pestilence, and the taker runs presently mad.] **God help the noble Claudio! If he have caught the Benedick, it will cost him a thousand pound ere 'a be cured.**

100

[MESSENGER　I will hold friends with you, lady.

BEATRICE　Do, good friend.

LEONATO　You will never run mad, niece.

BEATRICE　No, not till a hot January.]

110

MESS.　**Don Pedro is approached.**

Enter DON PEDRO, DON JOHN, CLAUDIO, BENEDICK and BALTHASAR.

D. PEDRO　**Good Signior Leonato, you are come to meet your trouble.** [The fashion of the world is to avoid cost, and you encounter it.]

LEONATO　**Never came trouble to my house in the likeness of your Grace.** [For trouble being gone, comfort should remain; but when you depart from me, sorrow abides and happiness takes his leave.]

120

D. PEDRO   **You embrace your charge too willingly. -- I think this is your daughter?**

LEONATO   **Her mother hath many times told me so.**

BENEDICK   **Were you in doubt, sir, that you asked her?**

130   **LEONATO**   **Signior Benedick, no, for then were you a child.**

D. PEDRO   [You have it full, Benedick. We may guess by this what you are, being a man. Truly, the lady fathers herself.] **Be happy, lady, for you are like an honourable father.**

BENEDICK   **If Signior Leonato be her father, she would not have his head on her shoulders for all Messina, as like him as she is.**

BEATRICE   **I wonder that you will still be talking, Signior**
140   **Benedick. Nobody marks you.**

BENEDICK   **What, my dear Lady Disdain, are you yet living?**

BEATRICE   **Is it possible disdain should die while she hath such meet food to feed it as Signior Benedick? Courtesy itself must convert to disdain, if you come in her presence.**

BENEDICK   **Then is courtesy a turncoat. But it is certain I am loved of all ladies, only you excepted. And I would I could find in**
150   **my heart that I had not a hard heart, for, truly, I love none.**

BEATRICE   **A dear happiness to women.** [They would else have been troubled with a pernicious suitor. I thank God and my cold blood, I am of your humour for that.] **I had rather hear my dog bark at a crow than a man swear he loves me.**

BENEDICK   **God keep your ladyship still in that mind. So some gentleman or other shall 'scape a predestinate scratched face.**

160   **BEATRICE**   **Scratching could not make it worse, an 'twere such a face as yours were.**

[BENEDICK   Well, you are a rare parrot-teacher.

BEATRICE   A bird of my tongue is better than a beast of yours.]

BENEDICK   **I would my horse had the speed of your tongue --** [and so good a continuer.] **But keep your way, in God's name, I have done.**

170   **BEATRICE**   **You always end with a jade's trick. I know you of old.**

D. PEDRO   [That is the sum of all, Leonato.--] **Signior Claudio and Signior Benedick, my dear friend Leonato hath invited you all.** [I tell him we shall stay here at the least a month, and he heartily prays some occasion may detain us longer. I dare swear he is no hypocrite, but prays from his heart.]

LEONATO   [If you swear, my lord, you shall not be forsworn.] *(To DON JOHN)* [Let me bid you welcome, my lord.] **Being reconciled to the Prince your brother, I owe you all duty.**
180
DON JOHN   **I thank you. I am not of many words, but I thank you.**

LEONATO   Please it your Grace lead on?

D. PEDRO   Your hand, Leonato. We will go together.

Exeunt all except BENEDICK and CLAUDIO.

190 **CLAUDIO**   Benedick, didst thou note the daughter of Signior Leonato?

BENEDICK   I noted her not, but I looked on her.

CLAUDIO   Is she not a modest young lady?

BENEDICK   Do you question me, as an honest man should do, for my simple true judgment? Or would you have me speak after my custom, as being a professed tyrant to their sex?

200 **CLAUDIO**   No, I pray thee, speak in sober judgment.

BENEDICK   Why, i' faith, methinks she's too low for a high praise, too brown for a fair praise and too little for a great praise. Only this commendation I can afford her, that were she other than she is, she were unhandsome. [And being no other but as she is, I do not like her.]

CLAUDIO   Thou thinkest I am in sport. I pray thee tell me truly how thou likest her.

210 **BENEDICK**   Would you buy her, that you inquire after her?

CLAUDIO   Can the world buy such a jewel?

BENEDICK   Yea, and a case to put it into. [But speak you this with a sad brow? Or do you play the flouting Jack, to tell us Cupid is a good hare-finder and Vulcan a rare carpenter? Come, in what key shall a man take you, to go in the song?]

CLAUDIO   In mine eye she is the sweetest lady that ever I looked on.
220

BENEDICK   I can see yet without spectacles, and I see no such matter. There's her cousin – an she were not possessed with a fury – exceeds her as much in beauty as the first of May doth the last of December. But I hope you have no intent to turn husband, have you?

CLAUDIO   I would scarce trust myself, though I had sworn the contrary, if Hero would be my wife.

230 **BENEDICK**   Is't come to this? [In faith, hath not the world one man but he will wear his cap with suspicion?] **Shall I never see a bachelor of three-score again?** [Go to, i' faith. An thou wilt needs thrust thy neck into a yoke, wear the print of it and sigh away Sundays.] **– Look, Don Pedro is returned to seek you.**

Enter DON PEDRO.

D. PEDRO   What secret hath held you here, that you followed not to Leonato's?

240 **BENEDICK**   I would your Grace would constrain me to tell.

D. PEDRO   I charge thee on thy allegiance.

BENEDICK   You hear, Count Claudio? I can be secret as a dumb man, [I would have you think so,] **but — on my allegiance, mark you this, on my allegiance —   he is in love. With who? Now that is your Grace's part. Mark how short his answer is: with Hero, Leonato's short daughter.**

250   [CLAUDIO   If this were so, so were it uttered.

BENEDICK   Like the old tale, my lord, 'It is not so, nor 'twas not so, but, indeed, God forbid it should be so.'

CLAUDIO   If my passion change not shortly, God forbid it should be otherwise.]

D. PEDRO   Amen if you love her, for the lady is very well worthy.

CLAUDIO   You speak this to fetch me in, my lord.
260

D. PEDRO   By my troth, I speak my thought.

CLAUDIO   And, in faith, my lord, I spoke mine.

BENEDICK   And, by my two faiths and troths, my lord, I spoke mine.

CLAUDIO   That I love her, I feel.

270   **D. PEDRO   That she is worthy, I know.**

BENEDICK   That I neither feel how she should be loved, nor know how she should be worthy, is the opinion that fire cannot melt out of me. I will die in it at the stake.

D. PEDRO   Thou wast ever an obstinate heretic in the despite of beauty.

[CLAUDIO   And never could maintain his part but in the force of his will.]
280

BENEDICK   That a woman conceived me, I thank her, that she brought me up, I likewise give her most humble thanks, but [that I will have a recheat winded in my forehead, or hang my bugle in an invisible baldrick, all women shall pardon me:] **because I will not do them the wrong to mistrust any, I will do myself the right to trust none; and the fine is** [-- for the which I may go the finer --] **I will live a bachelor.**

D. PEDRO   I shall see thee, ere I die, look pale with love.

290   **BENEDICK   With anger, with sickness, or with hunger, my lord, not with love.** [Prove that ever I lose more blood with love than I will get again with drinking, pick out mine eyes with a ballad-maker's pen and hang me up at the door of a brothel-house for the sign of blind Cupid.]

D. PEDRO   Well, if ever thou dost fall from this faith, thou wilt prove a notable argument.

BENEDICK   If I do, hang me in a bottle like a cat and shoot at me.
[And he that hits me, let him be clapped on the shoulder, and called Adam.]
300

D. PEDRO   [Well, as time shall try...] **'In time the savage bull doth bear the yoke.'**

73

BENEDICK **The savage bull may, but if ever the sensible Benedick bear it, pluck off the bull's horns and set them in my forehead. And** [let me be vilely painted, and] **in such great letters as they write, 'Here is good horse to hire,' let them signify under my sign: 'Here you may see Benedick the married man.'**

310   [CLAUDIO   If this should ever happen, thou wouldst be horn-mad.

        D. PEDRO   Nay, if Cupid have not spent all his quiver in Venice, thou wilt quake for this shortly.

        BENEDICK   I look for an earthquake too, then.]

D. PEDRO   [Well, you temporize with the hours.] **In the meantime, good Signior Benedick, repair to Leonato's. Commend me to him and tell him I will not fail him at supper, for indeed he hath made**
320   **great preparation.**

BENEDICK **I have almost matter enough in me for such an embassage ...** [and so I commit you --

        CLAUDIO   To the tuition of God. From my house, if I had it --

        DON PEDRO   The sixth of July. -- *Your loving friend, Benedick.*

        BENEDICK   Nay, mock not, mock not. The body of your discourse is sometime
330   guarded with fragments, and the guards are but slightly basted on neither. Ere you flout old ends any further, examine your conscience.] **And so I leave you.**   *(Exit)*

CLAUDIO   **My liege, your Highness now may do me good.**

D. PEDRO   **My love is thine to teach. Teach it but how,**
[And thou shalt see how apt it is to learn
Any hard lesson that may do thee good.]

CLAUDIO   **Hath Leonato any son, my lord?**
340

D. PEDRO   **No child but Hero. She's his only heir. Dost thou affect her, Claudio?**

CLAUDIO   **O, my lord,**
When you went onward on this ended action,
I looked upon her with a soldier's eye,
That liked, but had a rougher task in hand
Than to drive liking to the name of love.
But now I am returned and that war-thoughts
350   **Have left their places vacant, in their rooms**
Come thronging soft and delicate desires,
All prompting me how fair young Hero is ...
[Saying I liked her ere I went to wars.]

D. PEDRO   [Thou wilt be like a lover presently
And tire the hearer with a book of words.]
If thou dost love fair Hero, cherish it,
And I will break with her and with her father,
And thou shalt have her. Was't not to this end
360   **That thou began'st to twist so fine a story?**

CLAUDIO   **How sweetly you do minister to love,**

That know love's grief by his complexion.
[But lest my liking might too sudden seem,
I would have salved it with a longer treatise.]

D. PEDRO [What need the bridge much broader than the flood?
The fairest grant is the necessity.
Look, what will serve is fit. 'Tis once, thou lovest,]

370   **And I will fit thee with the remedy.**
I know we shall have revelling tonight ...
I will assume thy part in some disguise
And tell fair Hero I am Claudio,
And in her bosom I'll unclasp my heart
And take her hearing prisoner with the force
And strong encounter of my amorous tale.
Then after to her father will I break,
And the conclusion is, she shall be thine.
In practice let us put it presently.   *(Exeunt)*

Scene 2   *[A room in Leonato's house.]*
              Enter LEONATO and ANTONIO, meeting.

LEONATO   **How now, brother!** [Where is my cousin, your son? Hath he provided this music?]

ANTONIO   [He is very busy about it. But ...] **Brother, I can tell you strange news that you yet dreamt not of.**

10   [LEONATO   Are they good?

ANTONIO   [As the event stamps them: but they have a good cover, they show well outward.] **The Prince and Count Claudio, walking in a thick-pleached alley in mine orchard, were thus much overheard by a man of mine. The Prince discovered to Claudio that he loved my niece, your daughter, and meant to acknowledge it this night in a dance. And if he found her accordant, he meant to take the present time by the top and instantly break with you of it.**

20   **LEONATO**   **Hath the fellow any wit that told you this?**

ANTONIO   **A good sharp fellow. I will send for him, and question him yourself.**

LEONATO   **No, no...** [we will hold it as a dream till it appear itself.] **But I will acquaint my daughter withal, that she may be the better prepared for an answer, if peradventure this be true. Go you and tell her of it.** *[Enter ATTENDANTS)* Cousins, you know what you have to do. O, I cry you mercy, friend, go you with me, and I will use your skill. Good cousin, have a care this
30   busy time...]   *(Exeunt)*

Scene 3   *Enter DON JOHN and CONRADE.*

CONRADE   **What the good-year, my lord! Why are you thus out of measure sad?**

[DON JOHN   There is no measure in the occasion that breeds, therefore the sadness is without limit.

10

CONRADE   You should hear reason.

DON JOHN   And when I have heard it, what blessing brings it?

CONRADE   If not a present remedy, at least a patient sufferance.]

DON JOHN   [I wonder that thou, being, as thou sayest thou art, born under Saturn, goest about to apply a moral medicine to a mortifying mischief.] **I cannot hide what I am. I must be sad when I have cause and smile at no man's jests,** [eat when I have stomach and wait for no man's leisure, sleep when I am drowsy and tend on no man's business, laugh when I am merry and claw no man in his humour.]

20

CONRADE   **Yea, but you must not make the full show of this –** [till you may do it without controlment.] **You have of late stood out against your brother, and he hath ta'en you newly into his grace; where it is impossible you should take true root but by the fair weather that you make yourself.** [It is needful that you frame the season for your own harvest.]

DON JOHN   **I had rather be a canker in a hedge than a rose in his grace.** [And it better fits my blood to be disdained of all than to fashion a carriage to rob love from any.] **In this, though I cannot be said to be a flattering**

30   **honest man, it must not be denied but I am a plain-dealing villain.** [I am trusted with a muzzle and enfranchised with a clog; therefore I have decreed not to sing in my cage.] **If I had my mouth, I would bite; if I had my liberty, I would do my liking. In the meantime let me be that I am and seek not to alter me.**

[CONRADE   Can you make no use of your discontent?]

DON JOHN   [I make all use of it, for I use it only. --] **Who comes here?** *(Enter*

40   *BORACHIO)* **What news, Borachio?**

BORACHIO   **I came yonder from a great supper. The Prince your brother is royally entertained by Leonato, and I can give you intelligence of an intended marriage.**

DON JOHN   **Will it serve for any model to build mischief on? What is he for a fool that betroths himself to unquietness?**

BORACHIO   **Marry, it is your brother's right hand.**

50   **DON JOHN**   **Who, the most exquisite Claudio?**

BORACHIO   **Even he.**

DON JOHN   **A proper squire. And who, and who ...? Which way looks he?**

BORACHIO   **Marry, on Hero, the daughter and heir of Leonato.**

[DON JOHN   A very forward March-chick! How came you to this?

60

BORACHIO   Being entertained for a perfumer, as I was smoking a musty room, comes me the Prince and Claudio, hand in hand in sad conference. I whipt me behind the arras, and there heard it agreed upon that the Prince should woo Hero for himself, and having obtained her, give her to Count Claudio.]

DON JOHN   Come, come, let us thither. This may prove food to my displeasure. That young start-up hath all the glory of my overthrow. If I can cross him any way, I bless myself every way. You are both sure, and will assist me?

70

CONRADE   To the death, my lord.

DON JOHN   Let us to the great supper. [Their cheer is the greater that I am subdued. Would the cook were of my mind...] **Shall we go prove what's to be done?**

BORACHIO   We'll wait upon your lordship.   *(Exeunt)*

ACT TWO
Scene 1   *[A hall in Leonato's house.]*
             Enter LEONATO, ANTONIO, HERO, BEATRICE [and others].

LEONATO   Was not Count John here at supper?

ANTONIO   I saw him not.

BEATRICE   How tartly that gentleman looks! I never can see him
10   **but I am heart-burned an hour after.**

HERO   He is of a very melancholy disposition.

BEATRICE   He were an excellent man that were made just in the midway between him and Benedick. The one is too like an image and says nothing, and the other too like my lady's eldest son, evermore tattling.

LEONATO   Then half Signior Benedick's tongue in Count John's
20   **mouth, and half Count John's melancholy in Signior Benedick's face –**

BEATRICE   With a good leg and a good foot, uncle, and money enough in his purse, such a man would win any woman in the world, if 'a could get her goodwill.

LEONATO   By my troth, niece, thou wilt never get thee a husband, if thou be so shrewd of thy tongue.

30   [ANTONIO   In faith, she's too curst.

BEATRICE   Too curst is more than curst. I shall lessen God's sending that way, for it is said, 'God sends a curst cow short horns, but to a cow too curst he sends none'.

LEONATO   So, by being too curst, God will send you no horns.]

BEATRICE   [Just, if he send me no husband.] For the which blessing I am at him upon my knees every morning and evening. Lord, I could

40   **not endure a husband with a beard on his face. I had rather lie in the woollen.**

LEONATO   **You may light on a husband that hath no beard.**

BEATRICE   **What should I do with him? Dress him in my apparel and make him my waiting-gentlewoman? He that hath a beard is more than a youth, and he that hath no beard is less than a man. And he that is more than a youth is not for me, and he that is less than a man, I am not for him.** [Therefore, I will even take sixpence in earnest of the bear-ward, and lead his apes into hell.

50

LEONATO   Well, then, go you into hell?

BEATRICE   No, but to the gate; and there will the Devil meet me, like an old cuckold, with horns on his head, and say "Get you to heaven, Beatrice, get you to heaven. Here's no place for you maids." So deliver I up my apes, and away to Saint Peter for the heavens. He shows me where the bachelors sit, and there live we as merry as the day is long.]

ANTONIO   *(To Hero)* **Well, niece, I trust you will be ruled by your**
60   **father.**

BEATRICE   **Yes, faith, it is my cousin's duty to make curtsy and say "Father, as it please you." But yet for all that, cousin, let him be a handsome fellow, or else make another curtsy and say "Father, as it please me."**

LEONATO   **Well, niece, I hope to see you one day fitted with a husband.**

70   **BEATRICE**   **Not till God make men of some other metal than earth.** [Would it not grieve a woman to be overmastered with a pierce of valiant dust, to make an account of her life to a clod of wayward marl?] **No, uncle, I'll none. Adam's sons are my brethren, and, truly, I hold it a sin to match in my kindred.**

LEONATO   **Daughter, remember what I told you. If the Prince do solicit you in that kind, you know your answer.**

BEATRICE   **The fault will be in the music, cousin, if you be not**
80   **wooed in good time.** [If the Prince be too important, tell him there is measure in everything and so dance out the answer. For, hear me, Hero, wooing, wedding, and repenting, is as a Scotch jig, a measure, and a cinque-pace: the first suit is hot and hasty, like a Scotch jig, and full as fantastical; the wedding, mannerly-modest, as a measure, full of state and ancientry; and then comes repentance and, with his bad legs, falls into the cinque-pace faster and faster, till he sink into his grave.

LEONATO   Cousin, you apprehend passing shrewdly.

BEATRICE   I have a good eye, uncle: I can see a church by daylight.]
90

LEONATO   **The revellers are entering, brother. Make good room.**

All put on their masks. Enter DON PEDRO, CLAUDIO, BENEDICK, BALTHASAR, MARGARET, URSULA, masked, [MUSICIANS and, unmasked,] DON JOHN and BORACHIO.

D. PEDRO   **Lady, will you walk about with your friend?**

HERO   So you walk softly and look sweetly and say nothing, I
100   am yours for the walk – and especially when I walk away.

D. PEDRO   With me in your company?

HERO   I may say so, when I please.

D. PEDRO   And when please you to say so?

HERO   When I like your favour ... for God defend the lute
should be like the case.
110

[D. PEDRO   My visor is Philemon's roof. Within the house is Jove.

HERO   Why, then, your visor should be thatched.]

D. PEDRO   Speak low, if you speak love.   *(Draws her aside)*

BALTHASAR Well, I would you did like me.

MARGARET So would not I, for your own sake, for I have many ill
120   qualities.

BALTHASAR Which is one?

MARGARET I say my prayers aloud.

BALTHASAR I love you the better: the hearers may cry Amen.

MARGARET God match me with a good dancer!

130   [BALTHASAR   Amen.

MARGARET   And God keep him out of my sight when the dance is done! Answer,
clerk.

BALTHASAR   No more words. The clerk is answered.]   *(They step aside.)*

URSULA   I know you well enough. You are Signior Antonio.

ANTONIO   At a word, I am not.
140

URSULA   I know you by the waggling of your head.

ANTONIO   To tell you true, I counterfeit him.

URSULA   [You could never do him so ill-well, unless you were the very man.]
Here's his dry hand up and down. You are he, you are he.

ANTONIO   At a word, I am not.

150   **URSULA**   Come, come, do you think I do not know you by your
excellent wit? Can virtue hide itself? Go to, mum, you are he.
Graces will appear, and there's an end.   *(They step aside.)*

BEATRICE   Will you not tell me who told you so?

BENEDICK   No, you shall pardon me.

BEATRICE   Nor will you not tell me who you are?

160   **BENEDICK**   Not now.

BEATRICE   That I was disdainful, and that I had my good wit out of the 'Hundred Merry Tales' — well this was Signior Benedick that said so.

BENEDICK   What's he?

BEATRICE   I am sure you know him well enough.

170   **BENEDICK**   Not I, believe me.

BEATRICE   Did he never make you laugh?

BENEDICK   I pray you, what is he?

BEATRICE   Why, he is the Prince's jester, a very dull fool. Only his gift is in devising impossible slanders. None but libertines delight in him; and the commendation is not in his wit, but in his villainy; [for he both pleases men and angers them, and then they laugh at him and
180   beat him.] I am sure he is in the fleet. I would he had boarded me.

BENEDICK   When I know the gentleman, I'll tell him what you say.

BEATRICE   Do, do. He'll but break a comparison or two on me; which, peradventure not marked or not laughed at, strikes him into melancholy — and then there's a partridge wing saved, for the fool will eat no supper that night. *(Music)* We must follow the leaders.

190   [BENEDICK   In every good thing.

BEATRICE   Nay, if they lead to any ill, I will leave them at the next turning.]

Dance. Then exeunt all except DON JOHN, BORACHIO and CLAUDIO.

DON JOHN   Sure my brother is amorous on Hero and hath withdrawn her father to break with him about it. The ladies follow her and but one visor remains.

200   **BORACHIO**   And that is Claudio. I know him by his bearing.

DON JOHN   Are not you Signior Benedick?

CLAUDIO   You know me well. I am he.

DON JOHN   Signior, you are very near my brother in his love. He is enamoured on Hero. I pray you, dissuade him from her. She is no equal for his birth. You may do the part of an honest man in it.

210   **CLAUDIO**   How know you he loves her?

DON JOHN   I heard him swear his affection.

BORACHIO   So did I too. And he swore he would marry her tonight.

DON JOHN   Come, let us to the banquet.

Exeunt DON JOHN and BORACHIO.
220

CLAUDIO   Thus answer I in the name of Benedick,
But hear these ill news with the ears of Claudio.
'Tis certain so. The Prince woos for himself.

Friendship is constant in all other things
Save in the office and affairs of love.
Therefore, all hearts in love use their own tongues;
Let every eye negotiate for itself
And trust no agent; for beauty is a witch
Against whose charms faith melteth into blood.
230 [This is an accident of hourly proof,
Which I mistrusted not.] **Farewell, therefore, Hero!**

Enter BENEDICK.

BENEDICK   Count Claudio?

CLAUDIO   Yea, the same.

BENEDICK   Come, will you go with me?
240

CLAUDIO   Whither?

BENEDICK   [Even to the next willow, about your own business, Count.] **What fashion will you wear the garland of?** [About your neck, like an usurer's chain? Or under your arm, like a lieutenant's scarf?] **You must wear it one way, for the Prince hath got your Hero.**

CLAUDIO   I wish him joy of her.

250 **BENEDICK**   **Why, that's spoken like an honest drover.** [So they sell bullocks.] **But did you think the Prince would have served you thus?**

CLAUDIO   I pray you, leave me.

BENEDICK   Ho, now you strike like the blind man. 'Twas the boy that stole your meat, and you'll beat the post.

CLAUDIO   If it will not be, I'll leave you.   *(Exit)*

260 **BENEDICK   Alas, poor hurt fowl, now will he creep into sedges ... But that my Lady Beatrice should know me, and not know me! The Prince's fool – ha! It may be I go under that title because I am merry... yea, but so I am apt to do myself wrong ... I am not so reputed. It is the base, though bitter, disposition of Beatrice that puts the world into her person and so gives me out. – Well, I'll be revenged as I may.**

Enter DON PEDRO.

270 **D. PEDRO   Now, signior, where's the Count? Did you see him?**

BENEDICK   Troth, my lord, [I have played the part of Lady Fame.] **I found him here as melancholy as a lodge in a warren. I told him, and I think I told him true, that your Grace had got the good will of this young lady, and I offered him my company to a willow-tree,** [either to make him a garland, as being forsaken, or] **to bind him up a rod, as being worthy to be whipped.**

D. PEDRO   To be whipped? What's his fault?
280

BENEDICK   The flat transgression of a schoolboy, who, being overjoyed with finding a birds' nest, shows it his companion, and he steals it.

D. PEDRO   Wilt thou make a trust a transgression? The transgression is in the stealer.

BENEDICK   Yet it had not been amiss the rod had been [made, and the garland too; for the garland he might have worn himself, and the rod he might have]

290   **bestowed on you, who, as I take it, have stolen his birds' nest.**

D. PEDRO   I will but teach them to sing, and restore them to the owner.

BENEDICK   If their singing answer your saying, by my faith, you say honestly.

D. PEDRO   The Lady Beatrice hath a quarrel to you: the gentle-

300   man that danced with her told her she is much wronged by you.

BENEDICK   O, she misused me past the endurance of a block! An oak but with one green leaf on it would have answered her. My very visor began to assume life and scold with her. She told me, not thinking I had been myself, that I was the Prince's jester, that I was duller than a great thaw – [huddling jest upon jest with such impossible conveyance upon me that I stood like a man at a mark, with a whole army shooting at me.] **She speaks poniards, and every word stabs. If her breath were as terrible as her terminations, there were no living near her; she would infect to the north star.** [I would not marry her, though she were

310   endowed with all that Adam had left him before he transgressed. She would have made Hercules have turned spit, yea, and have cleft his club to make the fire too. Come, talk not of her. You shall find her the infernal Ate in good apparel. I would to God some scholar would conjure her; for certainly, while she is here, a man may live as quiet in hell as in a sanctuary; and people sin upon purpose, because they would go thither.] **So, indeed, all disquiet, horror and perturbation follows her.**

D. PEDRO   Look, here she comes.

Enter CLAUDIO, BEATRICE, HERO and LEONATO.

320

BENEDICK   Will your Grace command me any service to the world's end? I will go on the slightest errand now to the Antipodes that you can devise to send me on. I will fetch you a tooth-picker now from the furthest inch of Asia, [bring you the length of Prester John's foot, fetch you a hair off the great Cham's beard,] do you any embassage to the Pygmies, rather than hold three words' conference with this harpy. You have no employment for me?

D. PEDRO   None, but to desire your good company.

330

BENEDICK   O God, sir, here's a dish I love not. I cannot endure my Lady Tongue. *(Exit)*

D. PEDRO   Come, lady, come. You have lost the heart of Signior Benedick.

BEATRICE   Indeed, my lord, he lent it me awhile, and I gave him use for it – a double heart for his single one. Marry, once before he won it of me with false dice, therefore your Grace may well say

340   I have lost it.

D. PEDRO   You have put him down, lady, you have put him down.

BEATRICE   So I would not he should do me, my lord, lest I should prove the mother of fools. I have brought Count Claudio, whom you sent me to seek.

D. PEDRO   Why, how now, Count, wherefore are you sad?

350 **CLAUDIO**   Not sad, my lord.

D. PEDRO   How then, sick?

CLAUDIO   Neither, my lord.

BEATRICE   The Count is neither sad, nor sick, nor merry, nor well, but civil,   Count – civil as an orange, and something of that jealous complexion.

360 **D. PEDRO**   [I' faith, lady, I think your blazon to be true; though I'll be sworn, if he be so, his conceit is false.] **Here, Claudio, I have wooed in thy name, and fair Hero is won. I have broke with her father, and his good will obtained. Name the day of marriage, and God give thee joy!**

LEONATO   Count, take of me my daughter, and with her my fortunes. His Grace hath made the match, and all grace say Amen to it.

370 **BEATRICE**   Speak, Count, 'tis your cue.

CLAUDIO   Silence is the perfectest herald of joy. I were but little happy, if I could say how much. Lady, as you are mine, I am yours.
[I give away myself for you and dote upon the exchange.]

BEATRICE   Speak, cousin ... or, if you cannot, stop his mouth with a kiss, and let not him speak neither.

D. PEDRO   In faith, lady, you have a merry heart.

380 **BEATRICE**   Yea, my lord. I thank it, poor fool, it keeps on the windy side of care. My cousin tells him in his ear that he is in her heart.

CLAUDIO   And so she doth, cousin.

BEATRICE   [Good Lord, for alliance!] **Thus goes every one to the world but I, and I am sunburnt. I may sit in a corner and cry heigh-ho for a husband!**

390 **D. PEDRO**   Lady Beatrice, I will get you one.

BEATRICE   I would rather have one of your father's getting. Hath your Grace ne'er a brother like you? Your father got excellent husbands, if a maid could come by them.

D. PEDRO   Will you have me, lady?

BEATRICE   No, my lord, unless I might have another for working-days ...   your Grace is too costly to wear every day. – But, I
400 beseech your Grace, pardon me. I was born to speak all mirth and no matter.

D. PEDRO   Your silence most offends me, and to be merry best becomes you; for, out of question, you were born in a merry hour.

BEATRICE   No, sure, my lord, my mother cried. [But then there was a star danced, and under that was I born.] **Cousins, God give you joy!**

410

LEONATO   Niece, will you look to those things I told you of?

BEATRICE   I cry you mercy, uncle. By your Grace's pardon. *(Exit)*

D. PEDRO   By my troth, a pleasant-spirited lady.

LEONATO   There's little of the melancholy element in her, my Lord. She is never sad but when she sleeps. [And not ever sad then; for I have heard my daughter say, she hath often dreamed of unhappiness and waked herself with laughing.]

420   **D. PEDRO**   She cannot endure to hear tell of a husband.

LEONATO   O, by no means. She mocks all her wooers out of suit.

D. PEDRO   She were an excellent wife for Benedick.

LEONATO   O Lord, my lord, if they were but a week married, they would talk themselves mad.

430

D. PEDRO   Count Claudio, when mean you to go to church?

CLAUDIO   Tomorrow, my lord. Time goes on crutches till Love have all his rites.

LEONATO   Not till Monday, my dear son, which is hence a just seven-night; and a time too brief, too, to have all things answer my mind.

D. PEDRO   Come, you shake the head at so long a breathing. But, I warrant thee, Claudio, the time shall not go dully by us. I will in

440   the interim undertake one of Hercules' labours, which is, to bring Signior Benedick and the Lady Beatrice into a mountain of affection the one with the other. I would fain have it a match, and I doubt not but to fashion it, if you three will but minister such assistance as I shall give you direction.

LEONATO   My lord, I am for you, though it cost me ten nights' watchings.

450

CLAUDIO   And I, my lord.

D. PEDRO   And you too, gentle Hero?

HERO   I will do any modest office, my lord, to help my cousin to a good husband.

D. PEDRO   And Benedick is not the unhopefullest husband that I know. Thus far can I praise him: he is of a noble strain, of approved valour and confirmed honesty. I will teach you how to humour your cousin, that she shall fall in love with Benedick; and

460   I, with your two helps, will so practise on Benedick that, in despite of his quick wit and his queasy stomach, he shall fall in love with Beatrice. If we can do this, Cupid is no longer an archer. His

**glory shall be ours, for we are the only love-gods. Go in with me,
and I will tell you my drift.** *(Exeunt)*

Scene 2   *Enter DON JOHN and BORACHIO.*

DON JOHN   **It is so. The Count Claudio shall marry the daughter
of Leonato.**

BORACHIO   **Yea, my lord, but I can cross it.**

DON JOHN   **Any bar, any cross, any impediment will be
medicinable to me. I am sick in displeasure to him, and**
10   **whatsoever comes athwart his affection ranges evenly with mine.
How canst thou cross this marriage?**

[BORACHIO   Not honestly, my lord, but so covertly that no dishonesty shall appear in
me.

DON JOHN   Show me briefly how.]

**BORACHIO   I think I told your lordship a year since, how much I
am in the favour of Margaret, the waiting gentlewoman to Hero.**
20
DON JOHN   I remember.

**BORACHIO   I can, at any unseasonable instant of the night,
appoint her to look out at her lady's chamber window.**

DON JOHN   What life is in that, to be the death of this marriage?

**BORACHIO   The poison of that lies in you to temper. Go you to the
Prince your brother. Spare not to tell him that he hath wronged**
30   **his honour in marrying the renowned Claudio** [-- whose estimation do
you mightily hold up --] **to a contaminated stale, such a one as Hero.**

DON JOHN   What proof shall I make of that?

**BORACHIO   Proof enough to misuse the Prince, to vex Claudio, to
undo Hero and kill Leonato. Look you for any other issue?**

DON JOHN   Only to despite them I will endeavour anything.

40   **BORACHIO   Go then. Find me a meet hour to draw Don Pedro and
the Count Claudio alone. Tell them that you know that Hero loves
me.** [Intend a kind of zeal both to the Prince and Claudio, as -- in love of your brother's
honour, who hath made this match, and his friend's reputation, who is thus like to be
cozened with the semblance of a maid -- that you have discovered thus.] **They will
scarcely believe this without trial. Offer them instances, which
shall bear no less likelihood than to see me at her chamber-
window; hear me call Margaret Hero; hear Margaret term me
Claudio; and bring them to see this the very night before the
intended wedding** [-- for in the meantime I will so fashion the matter that Hero
50   shall be absent, and there shall appear such seeming truth of Hero's disloyalty that
jealousy shall be called assurance and all the preparation overthrown.]

DON JOHN   Grow this to what adverse issue it can, I will put it in practice.   Be cunning in the working this, and thy fee is a thousand ducats.

BORACHIO   Be you constant in the accusation, and my cunning shall not shame me.

60   **DON JOHN**   I will presently go learn their day of marriage.

Exeunt.

Scene 3   *[Leonato's orchard.]*
Enter BENEDICK.

BENEDICK   Boy!

Enter BOY.

BOY   Signior?

10   **BENEDICK**   In my chamber window lies a book.   Bring it hither to me in the orchard.

BOY   I am here already, sir.

BENEDICK   I know that, but I would have thee hence, and here again.   *(Exit BOY)* I do much wonder that one man, seeing how much another man is a fool when he dedicates his behaviours to love, will, after he hath laughed at such shallow follies in others, become the argument of his own scorn by falling in love – and
20   such a man is Claudio.   I have known when there was no music with him but the drum and the fife, [and now had he rather hear the tabour and the pipe.   I have known] when he would have walked ten mile a-foot to see a good armour... [and now will he lie ten nights awake, carving the fashion of a new doublet.]   He was wont to speak plain and to the purpose, like an honest man and a soldier; and now [is he turned orthography;] his words are a very fantastical banquet... [just so many strange dishes].   May I be so converted and see with these eyes?   I cannot tell.   I think not.   [I will not be sworn, but love may transform me to an oyster ... But I'll take my oath on it, till he have made an oyster of me, he shall never make me such a fool.]   One
30   woman is fair, yet I am well;   another is wise, yet I am well; another virtuous, yet I am well; but till all graces be in one woman, one woman shall not come in my grace.   Rich she shall be, that's certain; wise, or I'll none; virtuous, or I'll never cheapen her; fair, or I'll never look on her; mild, or come not near me; [noble, or not I for an angel; of good discourse,] an excellent musician, and her hair shall be of what colour it please God. – Ha, the Prince and Monsieur Love! I will hide me in the arbour.   *(Withdraws)*

40   *Enter DON PEDRO, CLAUDIO, LEONATO and BALTHASAR to music.*

D. PEDRO   Come, shall we hear this music?

CLAUDIO   Yea, my good lord.   How still the evening is,
As hushed on purpose to grace harmony!

D. PEDRO   See you where Benedick hath hid himself?

CLAUDIO O, very well, my lord. The music ended,
We'll fit the kid-fox with a pennyworth.

50

D. PEDRO Come, Balthasar, we'll hear that song again.

[BALTHASAR O, good my lord, tax not so bad a voice
To slander music any more than once.

DON PEDRO It is the witness still of excellency
To put a strange face on his own perfection.
I pray thee, sing, and let me woo no more.

60 BALTHASAR Because you talk of wooing, I will sing.
Since many a wooer doth commence his suit
To her he thinks not worthy, yet he woos,
Yet will he swear he loves.

DON PEDRO Now, pray thee, come.
Or, if thou wilt hold longer argument,
Do it in notes.

BALTHASAR Note this before my notes;
70 There's not a note of mine that's worth the noting.

DON PEDRO Why, these are very crotchets that he speaks;
Note, notes, forsooth, and nothing.]

Music.

BENEDICK Now, divine air, now is his soul ravished. Is it not
strange that sheeps' guts should hale souls out of men's bodies?
Well, a horn for my money, when all's done.

80
The Song.
BALTHASAR Sigh no more, ladies, sigh no more,
Men were deceivers ever;
One foot in sea and one on shore,
To one thing constant never.
Then sigh not so, but let them go,
And be you blithe and bonny,
Converting all your sounds of woe
Into Hey nonny, nonny.

90

[Sing no more ditties, sing no more,
Of dumps so dull and heavy;
The fraud of men was ever so,
Since summer first was leafy.
Then sigh not so, &c.]

D. PEDRO By my troth, a good song.

BALTHASAR And an ill singer, my lord.

100

D. PEDRO Ha, no, no, faith! Thou sing'st well enough for a shift.

BENEDICK *(Aside)* An he had been a dog that should have howled
thus, they would have hanged him. [And I pray God his bad voice bode no

87

mischief. I had as lief have heard the night-raven, come what plague could have come after it.]

D. PEDRO   Yea, marry, dost thou hear, Balthasar? I pray thee, get us some excellent music, for tomorrow night we would have it at
110   the Lady Hero's chamber-window.

BALTHASAR The best I can, my lord.

D. PEDRO   Do so.   Farewell.   *(Exit BALTHASAR [with MUSICIANS])* Come hither, Leonato. What was it you told me of today, that your niece Beatrice was in love with Signior Benedick?

CLAUDIO   O, ay. *(Aside to PEDRO)* Stalk on, stalk on, the fowl sits! – I did never think that lady would have loved any man.
120

LEONATO   No, nor I neither, but most wonderful that she should so dote on Signior Benedick, whom she hath in all outward behaviors seemed ever to abhor.

BENEDICK   Is't possible? Sits the wind in that corner?

LEONATO   By my troth, my lord, I cannot tell what to think of it but that she loves him [with an enraged affection. It is past the infinite of
130   thought.]

D. PEDRO   May be she doth but counterfeit.

CLAUDIO   Faith, like enough.

LEONATO   O God, counterfeit!   There was never counterfeit of passion came so near the life of passion as she discovers it.

[DON PEDRO   Why, what effects of passion shows she?]

140   **CLAUDIO**   *(Aside)* **Bait the hook well, this fish will bite.**

[LEONATO   What effects, my lord? She will sit you, you heard my daughter tell you how.

CLAUDIO   She did, indeed.]

D. PEDRO   [How, how, pray you?] **You amaze me. I would have thought her spirit had been invincible against all assaults of affection.**

150   **LEONATO**   I would have sworn it had, my lord – especially against Benedick.

BENEDICK   I should think this a gull, but that the white-bearded fellow speaks it.   Knavery cannot, sure, hide himself in such reverence.

[CLAUDIO   He hath ta'en the infection, hold it up.]

      D. PEDRO   Hath she made her affection known to Benedick?
160
      LEONATO   No, and swears she never will. That's her torment.

CLAUDIO   ['Tis true, indeed.   So your daughter says.] **"Shall I," says she, "that have so oft encountered him with scorn, write to him that I love him?"**

LEONATO   This says she now when she is beginning to write to him, for she'll be up twenty times a night; and there will she sit in her smock till she have writ a sheet of paper. My daughter tells us all.

170

CLAUDIO   Now you talk of a sheet of paper, I remember a pretty jest your daughter told us of.

LEONATO   O, when she had writ it and was reading it over, she found Benedick and Beatrice between the sheet?

CLAUDIO   That.

180   LEONATO   O, she tore the letter into a thousand halfpence, railed at herself, that she should be so immodest to write to one that she knew would flout her. "I measure him," says she, "by my own spirit, for I should flout him, if he writ to me. Yea, though I love him, I should."

CLAUDIO   Then down upon her knees she falls, weeps, sobs, beats her heart, tears her hair, prays, curses: "O sweet Benedick, God give me patience!"

190   LEONATO   **She doth indeed, my daughter says so.** [And the ecstasy hath so much overborne her that my daughter is sometime afeared she will do a desperate outrage to herself. It is very true.]

D. PEDRO   It were good that Benedick knew of it by some other, if she will not discover it.

CLAUDIO   To what end? He would make but a sport of it and torment the poor lady worse.

200   D. PEDRO   [An he should, it were an alms to hang him.] **She's an excellent sweet lady. And, out of all suspicion, she is virtuous.**

CLAUDIO   And she is exceeding wise.

D. PEDRO   In every thing but in loving Benedick.

LEONATO   [O, my lord, wisdom and blood combating in so tender a body, we have ten proofs to one that blood hath the victory.] **I am sorry for her, as I have just cause, being her uncle and her guardian.**

210

D. PEDRO   [I would she had bestowed this dotage on me. I would have daffed all other respects and made her half myself.] **I pray you, tell Benedick of it, and hear what 'a will say.**

LEONATO   Were it good, think you?

CLAUDIO   Hero thinks surely she will die. For she says she will die, if he love her not. And she will die, ere she make her love known. [And she will die, if he woo her, rather than she will bate one breath of her

220   accustomed crossness.]

D. PEDRO   She doth well. If she should make tender of her love, 'tis very possible he'll scorn it. For the man, as you know all, hath a contemptible spirit.

CLAUDIO   He is a very proper man ...

89

[D. PEDRO   He hath indeed a good outward happiness.]

230   **CLAUDIO**   [Before God!] **– And, in my mind, very wise.**

D. PEDRO   He doth indeed show some sparks that are like wit.

CLAUDIO   And I take him to be valiant.

D. PEDRO   As Hector, I assure you. [And in the managing of quarrels you may say he is wise; for either he avoids them with great discretion, or undertakes them with a most Christian-like fear.

240   LEONATO   If he do fear God, 'a must necessarily keep peace. If he break the peace, he ought to enter into a quarrel with fear and trembling.]

D. PEDRO   [And so will he do; for the man doth fear God, howsoever it seems not in him by some large jests he will make. Well I am sorry for your niece.] **Shall we go seek Benedick, and tell him of her love?**

CLAUDIO   Never tell him, my lord. Let her wear it out with good counsel.

250   **LEONATO   Nay, that's impossible. She may wear her heart out first.**

D. PEDRO   Well, we will hear further of it by your daughter. Let it cool the while. I love Benedick well; and I could wish he would modestly examine himself, to see how much he is unworthy so good a lady.

LEONATO   My lord, will you walk? Dinner is ready.

260   **CLAUDIO   (Aside) If he do not dote on her upon this, I will never trust my expectation.**

D. PEDRO   (Aside) Let there be the same net spread for her. And that must your daughter and her gentlewomen carry. The sport will be, when they hold one an opinion of another's dotage – [and no such matter.] **That's the scene that I would see, which will be merely a dumb-show. Let us send her to call him in to dinner.**

Exeunt DON PEDRO, CLAUDIO and LEONATO.

270

BENEDICK   (Coming forward) This can be no trick: the conference was sadly borne ... [they have the truth of this from Hero, they seem to pity the lady, it seems her affections have their full bent ... Love me? Why, it must be requited.] **I hear how I am censured. They say I will bear myself proudly, if I perceive the love come from her. They say too that she will rather die than give any sign of affection. I did never think to marry ... I must not seem proud. Happy are they that hear their detractions and can put them to mending** ... [They say the lady is fair -- 'tis a truth, I can bear them witness... And virtuous -- 'tis so, I cannot reprove it. And wise -- but for loving me. By my troth, it is no addition to her wit, nor no great argument of her folly, for I will be horribly in love with her.] **I may chance have some odd quirks and remnants of wit broken on me, because I have railed so long against marriage, but doth not the appetite alter? A man loves the meat in his youth that he cannot endure in his age.** [Shall quips and sentences and these paper bullets of the brain awe a man from the career of his humour?]

No, the world must be peopled. When I said I would die a bachelor, I did not think I should live till I were married. – Here comes Beatrice. By this day, she's a fair lady! I do spy some marks of love in her.

290

Enter BEATRICE.

BEATRICE   Against my will I am sent to bid you come in to dinner.

BENEDICK   Fair Beatrice, I thank you for your pains.

BEATRICE   [I took no more pains for those thanks than you take pains to thank me.] **If it had been painful, I would not have come.**

300

BENEDICK   You take pleasure then in the message?

BEATRICE   Yea, just so much as you may take upon a knife's point – [and choke a daw withal. You have no stomach, signior?] **Fare you well.**   *(Exit)*

BENEDICK   Ha! "Against my will I am sent to bid you come in to dinner." There's a double meaning in that. ["I took no more pains for those thanks than you took pains to thank me." That's as much as to say, 'Any pains that I take for you is as easy as thanks'.] **If I do not take pity of her, I am a**

310   **villain.** [If I do not love her, I am a Jew.] **I will go get her picture.**   *(Exit)*

ACT THREE
Scene 1   *[Leonato's garden.]*
Enter HERO, MARGARET and URSULA.

HERO   Good Margaret, run thee to the parlour.
There shalt thou find my cousin Beatrice
Proposing with the Prince and Claudio.
Whisper her ear and tell her I and Ursula
Walk in the orchard, and our whole discourse
10   **Is all of her.** [Say that thou overheard'st us,
And bid her steal into the pleachèd bower,
Where honeysuckles, ripened by the sun,
Forbid the sun to enter, like favourites
Made proud by princes, that advance their pride
Against that power that bred it.] **There will she hide her**
To listen our purpose. This is thy office.
Bear thee well in it and leave us alone.

MARGARET   I'll make her come, I warrant you, presently.   *(Exit)*
20

HERO   Now, Ursula, when Beatrice doth come,
As we do trace this alley up and down,
Our talk must only be of Benedick.
When I do name him, let it be thy part
To praise him more than ever man did merit.
My talk to thee must be how Benedick
Is sick in love with Beatrice. [Of this matter

Is little Cupid's crafty arrow made,
That only wounds by hearsay.] *(Enter BEATRICE, behind)* **Now begin,**
30   **For look where Beatrice, like a lapwing, runs**
Close by the ground, to hear our conference ...

URSULA   **The pleasant'st angling is to see the fish**
Cut with her golden oars the silver stream,
And greedily devour the treacherous bait.
[So angle we for Beatrice, who even now
Is couchèd in the woodbine coverture.
Fear you not my part of the dialogue.]

40   **HERO**   [Then go we near her, that her ear lose nothing
Of the false sweet bait that we lay for it.]   *(Moving to where Beatrice hides:)*
... No, truly, Ursula, she is too disdainful.
[I know her spirits are as coy and wild
As haggards of the rock.]

URSULA   **But are you sure**
That Benedick loves Beatrice so entirely?

HERO   **So says the Prince and my new-trothèd lord.**
50

URSULA   **And did they bid you tell her of it, madam?**

HERO   **They did entreat me to acquaint her of it;**
But I persuaded them, if they loved Benedick,
To wish him wrestle with affection,
And never to let Beatrice know of it.

URSULA   **Why did you so? Doth not the gentleman**
Deserve as full as fortunate a bed
60   **As ever Beatrice shall couch upon?**

HERO   **O god of love! I know he doth deserve**
As much as may be yielded to a man;
But Nature never framed a woman's heart
Of prouder stuff than that of Beatrice.
Disdain and scorn ride sparkling in her eyes,
Misprising what they look on; and her wit
Values itself so highly that to her
All matter else seems weak. She cannot love,
70   **Nor take no shape nor project of affection,**
She is so self-endeared.

URSULA   **Sure, I think so;**
And therefore certainly it were not good
She knew his love, lest she make sport at it.

HERO   **Why, you speak truth. I never yet saw man,**
How wise, how noble, young, how rarely featured,
But she would spell him backward. [If fair-faced,
80   She would swear the gentleman should be her sister;
If black, why, Nature, drawing of an antique,
Made a foul blot; if tall, a lance ill-headed;
If low, an agate very vilely cut;
If speaking, why, a vane blown with all winds;

If silent, why, a block moved with none.
So turns she every man the wrong side out
And never gives to truth and virtue that
Which simpleness and merit purchaseth.]

90 **URSULA**   **Sure, sure, such carping is not commendable.**

HERO   [No, not to be so odd and from all fashions
As Beatrice is, cannot be commendable.]
**But who dare tell her so? If I should speak,
She would mock me into air. O, she would laugh me
Out of myself, press me to death with wit.
Therefore let Benedick, like covered fire,
Consume away in sighs, waste inwardly.
It were a better death than die with mocks,**
100 **Which is as bad as die with tickling.**

URSULA   **Yet tell her of it, hear what she will say.**

HERO   **No, rather I will go to Benedick
And counsel him to fight against his passion.
And, truly, I'll devise some honest slanders
To stain my cousin with. One doth not know
How much an ill word may empoison liking.**

110 **URSULA**   **O, do not do your cousin such a wrong!
She cannot be so much without true judgment
(Having so swift and excellent a wit
As she is prized to have) as to refuse
So rare a gentleman as Signior Benedick.**

HERO   **He is the only man of Italy,
Always excepted my dear Claudio.**

[**URSULA**   I pray you, be not angry with me, madam,
120 Speaking my fancy. Signior Benedick,
For shape, for bearing, argument and valour,
Goes foremost in report through Italy.

HERO   Indeed, he hath an excellent good name.]

URSULA   [His excellence did earn it, ere he had it.]
When are you married, madam?

HERO   **Why, every day, tomorrow! Come, go in.**
130 **I'll show thee some attires, and have thy counsel
Which is the best to furnish me tomorrow.**

URSULA   *(Aside)*
She's limed, I warrant you! We've caught her, madam.

HERO   **If it proves so, then loving goes by haps.
Some Cupid kills with arrows, some with traps.**

Exeunt HERO and URSULA.
140

BEATRICE   *(Coming forward)*
     **What fire is in mine ears? Can this be true?
     Stand I condemned for pride and scorn so much?**

Contempt, farewell, and maiden pride, adieu!
No glory lives behind the back of such.
And, Benedick, love on! I will requite thee,
Taming my wild heart to thy loving hand.
If thou dost love, my kindness shall incite thee
To bind our loves up in a holy ban.
150   [For others say thou dost deserve, and I
Believe it better than reportingly.]   *(Exit)*

Scene 2   *[A room in Leonato's house.]*
Enter DON PEDRO, CLAUDIO, BENEDICK and LEONATO.

D. PEDRO   I do but stay till your marriage be consummate, and then go I toward Arragon.

CLAUDIO   I'll bring you thither, my lord, if you'll vouchsafe me.

10   **D. PEDRO**   Nay, that would be as great a soil in the new gloss of your marriage as to show a child his new coat and forbid him to wear it. I will only be bold with Benedick for his company, for, from the crown of his head to the sole of his foot, he is all mirth. [He hath twice or thrice cut Cupid's bow-string and the little hangman dare not shoot at him. He hath a heart as sound as a bell and his tongue is the clapper, for what his heart thinks his tongue speaks.]

BENEDICK   Gallants, I am not as I have been.

20   **LEONATO**   So say I. Methinks you are sadder.

CLAUDIO   I hope he be in love.

D. PEDRO   Hang him, truant! There's no true drop of blood in him to be truly touched with love. If he be sad, he wants money.

BENEDICK   I have the toothache.

30   **D. PEDRO**   Draw it!

[BENEDICK   Hang it!

CLAUDIO   You must hang it first, and draw it afterwards.

D. PEDRO   What, sigh for the toothache?

LEONATO   Where is but a humour or a worm.]

40   **BENEDICK**   Well every one can master a grief but he that has it.

CLAUDIO   Yet say I, he is in love.

D. PEDRO   There is no appearance of fancy in him... [unless it be a fancy that he hath to strange disguises as: to be a Dutchman today, a Frenchman tomorrow; or in the shape of two countries at once as: a German from the waist downward (all slops), and a Spaniard from the hip upward (no doublet). Unless he have a fancy to this foolery, as it appears he hath, he is no fool for fancy, as you would have it appear he is.]

CLAUDIO   If he be not in love with some woman, there is no
50   believing old signs. 'A brushes his hat o' mornings – what should
that bode?

D. PEDRO   Hath any man seen him at the barber's?

CLAUDIO   No, but the barber's man hath been seen with him,
and the old ornament of his cheek hath already stuffed tennis-
balls.

LEONATO   Indeed, he looks younger than he did, by the loss of a
60   beard.

[D. PEDRO   Nay, 'a rubs himself with civet. Can you smell him out by that?

CLAUDIO   That's as much as to say, the sweet youth's in love.

D. PEDRO   The greatest note of it is his melancholy.]

CLAUDIO   And when was he wont to wash his face?

70   [D. PEDRO   Yea, or to paint himself? For the which, I hear what they say of him.

CLAUDIO   Nay, but his jesting spirit … which is now crept into a lute-string and
now governed by stops.]

D. PEDRO   Indeed, that tells a heavy tale for him. Conclude,
conclude he is in love.

CLAUDIO   Nay, but I know who loves him.

80   **D. PEDRO**   That would I know too. I warrant, one that knows
him not.

CLAUDIO   Yes, and his ill conditions … and, in despite of all, dies
for him.

D. PEDRO   She shall be buried with her face upwards.

BENEDICK   Yet is this no charm for the toothache. Old signior,
walk aside with me. I have studied eight or nine wise words to
90   speak to you, which these hobby-horses must not hear.

Exeunt BENEDICK and LEONATO.

D. PEDRO   For my life, to break with him about Beatrice!

CLAUDIO   'Tis even so. Hero and Margaret have by this played
their parts with Beatrice, and then the two bears will not bite one
another when they meet.

100   *Enter DON JOHN.*

DON JOHN   My lord and brother, God save you!

D. PEDRO   Good den, brother.

DON JOHN   If your leisure served, I would speak with you.

D. PEDRO   In private?

110   **DON JOHN**   If it please you. Yet Count Claudio may hear, for what
I would speak of concerns him.

D. PEDRO   What's the matter?

DON JOHN   *(To Claudio)* **Means your lordship to be married tomorrow?**

D. PEDRO   You know he does.

120   **DON JOHN**   I know not that, when he knows what I know.

CLAUDIO   If there be any impediment, I pray you discover it.

DON JOHN   You may think I love you not. [Let that appear hereafter, and aim better at me by that I now will manifest. For my brother, I think he holds you well, and in dearness of heart hath holp to effect your ensuing marriage. Surely suit ill spent and labour ill bestowed.]

130   **D. PEDRO**   Why, what's the matter?

DON JOHN   [I came hither to tell you, and, circumstances shortened (for she has been too long a-talking of):] **The lady is disloyal.**

CLAUDIO   Who, Hero?

DON JOHN   Even she. Leonato's Hero, your Hero, every man's Hero.

140   **CLAUDIO**   Disloyal?

DON JOHN   [The word is too good to paint out her wickedness. I could say she were worse. Think you of a worse title, and I will fit her to it.] **Wonder not till further warrant. Go but with me tonight, you shall see her chamber-window entered, even the night before her wedding-day. If you love her then, tomorrow wed her. But it would better fit your honour to change your mind.**

CLAUDIO   May this be so?

150   **D. PEDRO**   I will not think it.

DON JOHN   If you dare not trust that you see, confess not that you know. If you will follow me, I will show you enough; and when you have seen more and heard more, proceed accordingly.

CLAUDIO   If I see any thing tonight why I should not marry her tomorrow in the congregation, where I should wed, there will I shame her.

160   **D. PEDRO**   And, as I wooed for thee to obtain her, I will join with thee to disgrace her.

DON JOHN   I will disparage her no farther till you are my witnesses. Bear it coldly but till midnight, and let the issue show itself.

[**D. PEDRO**   O day untowardly turned!

CLAUDIO   O mischief strangely thwarting!

170   **DON JOHN**   O plague right well prevented! So will you say when you have seen the sequel.]   *(Exeunt)*

Scene 3   *[A street.]*
               Enter DOGBERRY and VERGES with the Watch.

DOGBERRY Are you good men and true?

VERGES   Yea, or else it were pity but they should suffer salvation, body and soul.

DOGBERRY Nay, that were a punishment too good for them, [if they
should have any allegiance in them,] **being chosen for the Prince's watch.**

VERGES   Well, give them their charge, neighbour Dogberry.

DOGBERRY First, who think you the most desertless man to be constable?

1ˢᵗ WATCH.   Hugh Oatcake, sir, or George Seacole, for they can write and read.

DOGBERRY Come hither, neighbour Seacole. [God hath blessed you with
a good name. To be a well-favoured man is the gift of fortune, but to write and read
comes by nature.

2ⁿᵈ WATCH.   Both which, Master Constable --

DOGBERRY   You have. I knew it would be your answer. Well, for your favour, sir,
why, give God thanks, and make no boast of it. And for your writing and reading, let
that appear when there is no need of such vanity.] **You are thought here to be
the most senseless and fit man for the Constable of the Watch --
therefore bear you the lantern. This is your charge: you shall
comprehend all vagrom men; you are to bid any man stand, in the
Prince's name.**

2ⁿᵈ WATCH. How if 'a will not stand?

**DOGBERRY Why, then, take no note of him, but let him go. And
presently call the rest of the watch together and thank God you
are rid of a knave.**

**VERGES   If he will not stand when he is bidden, he is none of
the Prince's subjects.**

**DOGBERRY True, and they are to meddle with none but the
Prince's subjects. You shall also make no noise in the streets; for,
for the watch to babble and to talk is most tolerable and not to be
endured.**

**1ˢᵗ WATCH.   We will rather sleep than talk. We know what belongs
to a watch.**

**DOGBERRY Why, you speak like an ancient and most quiet
watchman, for I cannot see how sleeping should offend. Only, have
a care that your bills be not stolen. Well, you are to call at all the
ale-houses, and bid those that are drunk get them to bed.**

1ˢᵗ WATCH.   How if they will not?

DOGBERRY Why, then, let them alone till they are sober. [If they make you not then the better answer, you may say they are not the men you took them for.]

60

1st WATCH.   Well, sir.

DOGBERRY If you meet a thief, you may suspect him, by virtue of your office, to be no true man. And, for such kind of men, the less you meddle or make with them, why the more is for your honesty.

2nd WATCH.   If we know him to be a thief, shall we not lay hands on him?

70

DOGBERRY Truly, by your office, you may, but I think they that touch pitch will be defiled. The most peaceable way for you, if you do take a thief, is to let him show himself what he is and steal out of your company.

VERGES   You have been always called a merciful man, partner.

DOGBERRY Truly, I would not hang a dog by my will, much more a man who hath any honesty in him.

80

VERGES   If you hear a child cry in the night, you must call to the nurse and bid her still it.

2nd WATCH.   How if the nurse be asleep and will not hear us?

DOGBERRY Why, then, depart in peace, and let the child wake her with crying; for the ewe that will not hear her lamb when it baas will never answer a calf when he bleats.

90   **VERGES   'Tis very true.**

DOGBERRY This is the end of the charge. You, Constable, [are to present the Prince's own person...] **if you meet the Prince in the night, you may stay him.**

VERGES   Nay, by our lady, that I think 'a cannot.

DOGBERRY Five shillings to one on't, with any man that knows the statutes, he may stay him. – Marry, not without the Prince be

100   **willing; for, indeed, the watch ought to offend no man ... and it is an offence to stay a man against his will.**

VERGES   By'r lady, I think it be so.

DOGBERRY Ha, ha, ha! Well, masters, good night. [An there be any matter of weight chances, call up me. Keep your fellows' counsels and your own, and good night.] **– Come, neighbour.**

2nd WATCH.   Well, masters, we hear our charge. Let us go sit here

110   **upon the church-bench till two, and then all to bed.**

DOGBERRY One word more, honest neighbours. I pray you watch about Signior Leonato's door; for, the wedding being there tomorrow, there is a great coil tonight. Adieu. Be vigitant, I beseech you.

Exeunt DOGBERRY and VERGES. Enter BORACHIO and CONRADE.

BORACHIO   **What Conrade!**

2nd WATCH.   *(Aside)* **Peace! Stir not.**

BORACHIO   **Conrade, I say!**

CONRADE   **Here, man. I am at thy elbow.**

BORACHIO   [Mass!] **And my elbow itched! I thought there would a scab follow.**

CONRADE   **I will owe thee an answer for that ... And now forward with thy tale.**

BORACHIO   **Stand thee close, then, under this penthouse, for it drizzles rain, and I will, like a true drunkard, utter all to thee.**

2nd WATCH.   *(Aside)* **Some treason, masters, yet stand close.**

BORACHIO   **Therefore know I have earned of Don John a thousand ducats.**

CONRADE   **Is it possible that any villainy should be so dear?**

BORACHIO   **Thou shouldst rather ask if it were possible any villainy should be so rich; for when rich villains have need of poor ones, poor ones may make what price they will.**

CONRADE   **I wonder at it.**

[BORACHIO   That shows thou art unconfirmed. Thou knowest that the fashion of a doublet, or a hat, or a cloak, is nothing to a man.

CONRADE   Yes, it is apparel.

BORACHIO   I mean, the fashion.

CONRADE   Yes, the fashion is the fashion.

BORACHIO   Tush! I may as well say the fool's the fool. But seest thou not what a deformed thief this fashion is?

1st WATCH.   *(Aside)* I know that Deformed. 'A has been a vile thief this seven year. 'A goes up and down like a gentleman. I remember his name.

BORACHIO   Didst thou not hear somebody?

CONRADE   No, 'twas the vane on the house.

BORACHIO   Seest thou not, I say, what a deformed thief this fashion is? How giddily 'a turns about all the hot bloods between fourteen and five-and-thirty? Sometimes fashioning them like Pharaoh's soldiers in the reeky painting, sometime like god Bel's priests in the old church window, sometime like the shaven Hercules in the smirched worm-eaten tapestry, where his codpiece seems as massy as his club?

CONRADE   All this I see, and I see that the fashion wears out more apparel than the man. But art not thou thyself giddy with the fashion too, that thou hast shifted out of thy tale into telling me of the fashion?]

BORACHIO   [Not so, neither.] **But know that I have tonight wooed Margaret, the Lady Hero's gentlewoman, by the name of Hero. She leans me out at her mistress' chamber window, bids me a thousand**

times goodnight – I tell this tale vilely ... I should first tell thee how the Prince, Claudio and my master, planted and placed and possessed by my master Don John, saw afar off in the orchard this amiable encounter.

CONRADE   And thought they Margaret was Hero?

BORACHIO   Two of them did, the Prince and Claudio. But the devil my master knew she was Margaret; and partly by his oaths, [which first possessed them, partly by the dark night, which did deceive them,] **but chiefly by my villainy – which did confirm any slander that Don John had made – away went Claudio enraged, swore he would meet her, as he was appointed, next morning at the temple, and there, before the whole congregation, shame her with what he saw o'er night and send her home again without a husband.**

190

1ˢᵗ WATCH.   We charge you, in the Prince's name, stand!

2ⁿᵈ WATCH. Call up the right Master Constable. We have here recovered the most dangerous piece of lechery that ever was known in the commonwealth.

200

[1ˢᵗ WATCH.   And one Deformed is one of them. I know him, 'a wears a lock.

CONRADE   Masters, masters --

2ⁿᵈ WATCH.   You'll be made bring Deformed forth, I warrant you.]

CONRADE   Masters –

210

1ˢᵗ WATCH.   Never speak. We charge you let us obey you to go with us.

[BORACHIO   We are like to prove a goodly commodity, being taken up of these men's bills.]

CONRADE   [A commodity in question, I warrant you.] **Come, we'll obey you.**

(Exeunt)

Scene 4   *[Hero's apartment.]*
             Enter HERO, MARGARET and URSULA.

HERO   **Good Ursula, wake my cousin Beatrice, and desire her to rise.**

URSULA   **I will, lady.**

HERO   **And bid her come hither.**

10

URSULA   **Well.**   *(Exit)*

MARGARET   **Troth, I think your other *rebato* were better.**

HERO   **No, pray thee, good Meg, I'll wear this.**

MARGARET   **By my troth, 's not so good, and I warrant your cousin will say so.**

20 **HERO**   **My cousin's a fool, and thou art another. I'll wear none but this.**

MARGARET I like the new tire within excellently, if the hair were a thought browner ... and your gown's a most rare fashion, i' faith. I saw the Duchess of Milan's gown that they praise so.

HERO   **O, that exceeds, they say.**

MARGARET By my troth, 's but a night-gown in respect of yours:
30 **cloth o' gold, and cuts, and laced with silver, set with pearls...** [down sleeves, side sleeves, and skirts round underborne with a bluish tinsel.] **But for a fine, quaint, graceful and excellent fashion, yours is worth ten on 't.**

HERO   **God give me joy to wear it, for my heart is exceeding heavy.**

MARGARET 'Twill be heavier soon by the weight of a man.

HERO   **Fie upon thee! Art not ashamed?**
40

MARGARET Of what, lady? [Of speaking honourably? Is not marriage honourable in a beggar? Is not your lord honourable without marriage? I think you would have me say, 'saving your reverence, a husband'. An bad thinking do not wrest true speaking, I'll offend nobody.] **Is there any harm in 'the heavier for a husband'? None, I think, an it be the right husband and the right wife.** [Otherwise 'tis light, and not heavy.] **Ask my Lady Beatrice else – here she comes.**

Enter BEATRICE.
50

HERO   **Good morrow, coz.**

BEATRICE   **Good morrow, sweet Hero.**

HERO   **Why how now? Do you speak in the sick tune?**

BEATRICE   **I am out of all other tune, methinks.**

[MARGARET   Clap 's into 'Light o' love'. That goes without a burden. Do you sing it,
60 and I'll dance it.

BEATRICE   Ye light o' love, with your heels. Then, if your husband have stables enough, you'll see he shall lack no barns.

MARGARET   O illegitimate construction! I scorn that with my heels.]

BEATRICE   'Tis almost five o'clock, cousin. 'Tis time you were ready. By my troth, I am exceeding ill ... heigh-ho!

70 MARGARET   For a hawk, a horse, or a husband?

[BEATRICE   For the letter that begins them all, H.

MARGARET   Well, an you be not turned Turk, there's no more sailing by the star.]

BEATRICE   **What means the fool, trow?**

MARGARET Nothing I. But God send every one their heart's
80 **desire!**

HERO These gloves the Count sent me, they are an excellent perfume.

BEATRICE I am stuffed, cousin. I cannot smell.

MARGARET A maid, and stuffed! There's goodly catching of cold.

90

[BEATRICE O, God help me, God help me! How long have you professed apprehension?

MARGARET Even since you left it. Doth not my wit become me rarely?]

BEATRICE [It is not seen enough, you should wear it in your cap.] **By my troth, I am sick.**

MARGARET Get you some of this distilled *Carduus Benedictus*, and lay it to your heart. It is the only thing for a qualm.

100

HERO There thou prickest her with a thistle.

BEATRICE *Benedictus*? Why *Benedictus*? You have some moral in this *Benedictus*.

MARGARET Moral? No, by my troth, I have no moral meaning. [I meant, plain holy-thistle.] **You may think perchance that I think you are in love. Nay, by 'r lady, I am not such a fool to think** [what I list, nor I list not to think what I can, nor indeed I cannot think -- if I would think my heart out of thinking -- that you are in love or that you will be in love or] **that you can be in love. Yet Benedick** [was such another, and now is he become a man. He] **swore**

110

he would never marry, and yet now, in despite of his heart, he eats his meat without grudging. And how you may be converted I know not, but methinks you look with your eyes as other women do.

BEATRICE What pace is this that thy tongue keeps?

MARGARET Not a false gallop.

Enter URSULA.

120

URSULA Madam, withdraw. The Prince, the Count, Signior Benedick, Don John, and all the gallants of the town, are come to fetch you to church.

HERO Help to dress me, good coz, good Meg, good Ursula.

(Exeunt)

Scene 5 *[Another room in Leonato's house.]*
Enter LEONATO, with DOGBERRY and VERGES.

LEONATO What would you with me, honest neighbour?

DOGBERRY Marry, sir, I would have some confidence with you that decerns you nearly.

10

LEONATO Brief, I pray you, for you see it is a busy time with me.

DOGBERRY Marry, this it is, sir.

VERGES Yes, in truth it is, sir.

LEONATO   What is it, my good friends?

DOGBERRY   Goodman Verges, sir, speaks a little off the matter – an old man, sir, and his wits are not so blunt as, God help, I would desire they were ... but, in faith, honest as the skin between his 20   brows.

VERGES   Yes, I thank God I am as honest as any man living that is an old man and no honester than I.

DOGBERRY   Comparisons are odorous. [*Palabras*, neighbour Verges.]

LEONATO   Neighbours, you are tedious.

DOGBERRY   It pleases your worship to say so, but we are the poor 30   Duke's officers. But truly, for mine own part, if I were as tedious as a king, I could find it in my heart to bestow it all of your worship.

LEONATO   All thy tediousness on me, eh?

DOGBERRY   Yea, an 'twere a thousand pound more than 'tis. For I hear as good exclamation on your worship as of any man in the city – and though I be but a poor man, I am glad to hear it.

40   **VERGES**   And so am I.

LEONATO   I would fain know what you have to say.

VERGES   Marry, sir, our watch tonight, excepting your worship's presence, ha' ta'en a couple of as arrant knaves as any in Messina.

DOGBERRY   A good old man, sir – he will be talking! As they say, when the age is in, the wit is out. [God help us, it is a world to see! Well said 50   i' faith, neighbour Verges -- well, God's a good man.] **An two men ride of a horse, one must ride behind.** [An honest soul, i' faith, sir. By my troth he is, as ever broke bread, but God is to be worshipped.] **All men are not alike, alas, good neighbour.**

LEONATO   Indeed, neighbour, he comes too short of you.

DOGBERRY   Gifts that God gives!

60   **LEONATO**   I must leave you.

DOGBERRY   One word, sir. Our watch, sir, have indeed comprehended two auspicious persons, and we would have them this morning examined before your worship.

LEONATO   Take their examination yourself and bring it me. I am now in great haste, as it may appear unto you.

DOGBERRY   It shall be suffigance.

70   **LEONATO**   Drink some wine ere you go. Fare you well.

Enter A MESSENGER.

MESS.   My lord, they stay for you to give your daughter to her husband.

LEONATO   I'll wait upon them. I am ready.

Exeunt LEONATO and MESSENGER.

80

DOGBERRY Go, good partner, go, get you to Francis Seacole. Bid him bring his pen and inkhorn to the gaol. We are now to examination these men.

VERGES   And we must do it wisely.

DOGBERRY We will spare for no wit, I warrant you. [Here's that shall drive some of them to a non-come.] **Only get the learned writer to set down our excommunication and meet me at the jail.**   *(Exeunt)*

ACT FOUR
Scene 1   *[A church.]*
               Enter DON PEDRO, DON JOHN, LEONATO, FRIAR FRANCIS, CLAUDIO, BENEDICK, HERO and BEATRICE [with ATTENDANTS].

LEONATO   Come, Friar Francis, be brief. Only to the plain form of marriage, and you shall recount their particular duties afterwards.

10

F. FRANCIS You come hither, my lord, to marry this lady.

CLAUDIO   No.

LEONATO   To be married to her, Friar. You come to marry her.

F. FRANCIS Lady, you come hither to be married to this Count?

HERO   I do.

20

F. FRANCIS If either of you know any inward impediment why you should not be conjoined, I charge you, on your souls, to utter it.

CLAUDIO   Know you any, Hero?

HERO   None, my lord.

F. FRANCIS Know you any, Count?

30

LEONATO   I dare make his answer, none.

CLAUDIO   O, what men dare do! What men may do! What men daily do, not knowing what they do!

BENEDICK   How now? Interjections? [Why, then, some be of laughing, as, 'ah, ha, he!']

CLAUDIO   Stand thee by, Friar. Father, by your leave.

40   Will you with free and unconstrainèd soul
Give me this maid, your daughter?

LEONATO   As freely, son, as God did give her me.

CLAUDIO   And what have I to give you back, whose worth
May counterpoise this rich and precious gift?

D. PEDRO   Nothing, unless you render her again.

50   CLAUDIO   Sweet Prince, you learn me noble thankfulness.
There, Leonato, take her back again.
Give not this rotten orange to your friend.
She's but the sign and semblance of her honour.
Behold how like a maid she blushes here!
[O, what authority and show of truth
Can cunning sin cover itself withal!
Comes not that blood as modest evidence
To witness simple virtue?] Would you not swear,
All you that see her, that she were a maid,
60   By these exterior shows? But she is none.
She knows the heat of a luxurious bed.
Her blush is guiltiness, not modesty.

LEONATO   What do you mean, my lord?

CLAUDIO   Not to be married.
Not to knit my soul to an approvèd wanton.

LEONATO   Dear my lord, if you, in your own proof,
70   Have vanquished the resistance of her youth,
And made defeat of her virginity –

CLAUDIO   I know what you would say. If I have known her,
You will say she did embrace me as a husband,
And so extenuate the forehand sin.
No, Leonato,
I never tempted her with word too large,
But, as a brother to his sister, showed
Bashful sincerity and comely love.
80
HERO   And seemed I ever otherwise to you?

CLAUDIO   Out on thee, seeming! I will write against it:
[You seem to me as Diane in her orb,
As chaste as is the bud ere it be blown;
But] you are more intemp'rate in your blood
Than Venus, or those pampered animals
That rage in savage sensuality.

90   HERO   Is my lord well, that he doth speak so wide?

LEONATO   Sweet Prince, why speak not you?

D. PEDRO   What should I speak?
I stand dishonoured, that have gone about
To link my dear friend to a common stale.

LEONATO   Are these things spoken, or do I but dream?

100   **DON JOHN**   **Sir, they are spoken, and these things are true.**

BENEDICK   **This looks not like a nuptial.**

HERO   **'True.' — O God!**

CLAUDIO   **Leonato, stand I here?**
Is this the Prince? Is this the Prince's brother?
Is this face Hero's? Are our eyes our own?

110   **LEONATO**   **All this is so. But what of this, my lord?**

CLAUDIO   **Let me but move one question to your daughter:**
[And, by that fatherly and kindly power
That you have in her, bid her answer truly.

LEONATO   I charge thee do so, as thou art my child.

HERO   O, God defend me! How am I beset!
120   What kind of catechising call you this?

CLAUDIO   To make you answer truly to your name.

HERO   Is it not Hero? Who can blot that name
With any just reproach?]

CLAUDIO   [Marry, that can Hero.
Hero itself can blot out Hero's virtue.]
What man was he talked with you yesternight
Out at your window betwixt twelve and one?
130   **Now, if you are a maid, answer to this.**

HERO   **I talked with no man at that hour, my lord.**

D. PEDRO   **Why, then are you no maiden. — Leonato,**
I am sorry you must hear. Upon mine honour,
Myself, my brother and this grievèd count
Did see her, hear her, at that hour last night
Talk with a ruffian at her chamber-window
Who hath indeed, most like a liberal villain,
140   **Confessed the vile encounters they have had**
A thousand times in secret.

DON JOHN   **Fie, fie, they are**
Not to be named, my lord, not to be spoke of.
[There is not chastity enough in language
Without offence to utter them. Thus, pretty lady,
I am sorry for thy much misgovernment.]

CLAUDIO   **O Hero, what a Hero hadst thou been,**
150   **If half thy outward graces had been placed**
About thy thoughts and counsels of thy heart!
But fare thee well, most foul, most fair! Farewell,
Thou pure impiety and impious purity!
[For thee I'll lock up all the gates of love,
And on my eyelids shall conjecture hang,
To turn all beauty into thoughts of harm,
And never shall it more be gracious.]

LEONATO   Hath no man's dagger here a point for me?
160

HERO swoons.

BEATRICE   Why, how now, cousin, wherefore sink you down?

DON JOHN   Come, let us go. These things, come thus to light,
Smother her spirits up.

Exeunt DON PEDRO, DON JOHN and CLAUDIO.

170   **BENEDICK**   How doth the lady?

BEATRICE   Dead, I think. – Help, uncle!
Hero ... why, Hero! Uncle! Signior Benedick! Friar!

LEONATO   O Fate, take not away thy heavy hand.
Death is the fairest cover for her shame
That may be wished for.

BEATRICE   How now, cousin Hero?
180

F. FRANCIS   Have comfort, lady.

LEONATO   Dost thou look up?

F. FRANCIS   Yea, wherefore should she not?

LEONATO   Wherefore! Why, doth not every earthly thing
Cry shame upon her? Could she here deny
The story that is printed in her blood?
190   Do not live, Hero, do not ope thine eyes.
For, did I think thou wouldst not quickly die,
Thought I thy spirits were stronger than thy shames,
Myself would, on the rearward of reproaches,
Strike at thy life. Grieved I, I had but one?
[Chid I for that at frugal nature's frame?
O, one too much by thee! Why had I one?]
Why ever wast thou lovely in my eyes?
Why had I not with charitable hand
Took up a beggar's issue at my gates,
200   Who smirchèd thus and mired with infamy,
I might have said, 'No part of it is mine.
This shame derives itself from unknown loins'?
But mine and mine I loved, and mine I praised,
And mine that I was proud on [-- mine so much
That I myself was to myself not mine,
Valuing of her -- why, she, O, she is fallen
Into a pit of ink, that the wide sea
Hath drops too few to wash her clean again;
And salt too little which may season give
210   To her foul-tainted flesh!]

BENEDICK   Sir, sir, be patient.
For my part, I am so attired in wonder,
I know not what to say ...

BEATRICE   O, on my soul, my cousin is belied!

BENEDICK   Lady, were you her bedfellow last night?

220   **BEATRICE**   No, truly not — although, until last night,
I have this twelvemonth been her bedfellow.

LEONATO   Confirmed, confirmed! O, that is stronger made
Which was before barred up with ribs of iron!
Would the two princes lie, and Claudio lie,
Who loved her so, that, speaking of her foulness,
Washed it with tears? Hence from her, let her die!

F. FRANCIS   Hear me a little ...
230   For I have only been silent so long,
And given way unto this course of fortune,
By noting of the lady. I have marked
A thousand blushing apparitions
To start into her face, a thousand innocent shames
In angel whiteness beat away those blushes;
And in her eye there hath appeared a fire,
To burn the errors that these princes hold
Against her maiden truth. Call me a fool,
[Trust not my reading nor my observations,
240   Which with experimental seal doth warrant
The tenor of my book -- trust not my age,
My reverence, calling, nor divinity --]
If this sweet lady lie not guiltless here
Under some biting error.

LEONATO   Friar, it cannot be.
Thou seest that all the grace that she hath left
Is that she will not add to her damnation
A sin of perjury. She not denies it.
250   [Why seek'st thou then to cover with excuse
That which appears in proper nakedness?]

F. FRANCIS   Lady, what man is he you are accused of?

HERO   They know that do accuse me. I know none.
If I know more of any man alive
Than that which maiden modesty doth warrant,
Let all my sins lack mercy. O my father,
Prove you that any man with me conversed
260   At hours unmeet, or that I yesternight
Maintained the change of words with any creature,
Refuse me, hate me, torture me to death!

F. FRANCIS   There is some strange misprision in the Princes.

BENEDICK   Two of them have the very bent of honour;
And if their wisdoms be misled in this,
The practice of it lives in John the bastard,
Whose spirits toil in frame of villainies.
270

LEONATO   I know not. If they speak but truth of her,
These hands shall tear her. If they wrong her honour,
The proudest of them shall well hear of it.

Time hath not yet so dried this blood of mine,
Nor age so eat up my invention –
[Nor fortune made such havoc of my means,
Nor my bad life reft me so much of friends --
But they shall find, awaked in such a kind,
Both strength of limb and policy of mind,
280   Ability in means and choice of friends,
To quit me of them throughly.]

F. FRANCIS   Pause awhile,
And let my counsel sway you in this case.
Your daughter here the Princes left for dead.
Let her awhile be secretly kept in,
And publish it that she is dead indeed.
Maintain a mourning ostentation
And on your family's old monument
290   **Hang mournful epitaphs and do all rites**
That appertain unto a burial.

LEONATO   What shall become of this? What will this do?

F. FRANCIS Marry, this well carried shall on her behalf
Change slander to remorse. That is some good.
[But not for that dream I on this strange course,
But on this travail look for greater birth.]
She dying – as it must so be maintained,
300   [Upon the instant that she was accused --]
Shall be lamented, pitied and excused
Of every hearer. For it so falls out
That what we have we prize not to the worth
Whiles we enjoy it but, being lacked and lost,
Why, then we rack the value, then we find
The virtue that possession would not show us
Whiles it was ours. So will it fare with Claudio;
[When he shall hear she died upon his words,
The idea of her life shall sweetly creep
310   Into his study of imagination,]
And every lovely organ of her life
Shall come apparelled in more precious habit,
[More moving, delicate and full of life,
Into the eye and prospect of his soul,]
Than when she lived indeed. Then shall he mourn,
[If ever love had int'rest in his liver,]
And wish he had not so accused her –
No, though he thought his accusation true.
Let this be so, and doubt not but success
320   **Will fashion the event in better shape**
Than I can lay it down in likelihood.
[But if all aim but this be levelled false,
The supposition of the lady's death
Will quench the wonder of her infamy.]
And if it sort not well, you may conceal her,
As best befits her wounded reputation,
In some reclusive and religious life ...

[Out of all eyes, tongues, minds and injuries.]

330   **BENEDICK**   **Signior Leonato, let the Friar advise you.**
And though you know my inwardness and love
Is very much unto the Prince and Claudio,
Yet, by mine honour, I will deal in this
As secretly and justly as your soul
Should with your body.

  LEONATO   **Being that I flow in grief,**
The smallest twine may lead me.

340   [F. FRANCIS   'Tis well consented. Presently away;
                      For to strange sores strangely they strain the cure.
       (To Hero) Come, lady, die to live. This wedding-day
                      Perhaps is but prolonged. Have patience and endure.]

     Exeunt all but BENEDICK and BEATRICE.

  BENEDICK   **Lady Beatrice, have you wept all this while?**

  BEATRICE   **Yea, and I will weep a while longer.**
350

  BENEDICK   **I will not desire that.**

  BEATRICE   **You have no reason. I do it freely.**

  BENEDICK   **Surely I do believe your fair cousin is wronged.**

  BEATRICE   **Ah, how much might the man deserve of me that**
would right her!

360   **BENEDICK**   **Is there any way to show such friendship?**

  BEATRICE   **A very even way, but no such friend.**

  BENEDICK   **May a man do it?**

  BEATRICE   **It is a man's office, but not yours.**

  BENEDICK   **I do love nothing in the world so well as you. Is not**
that strange?
370

  BEATRICE   **As strange as the thing I know not. It were as**
possible for me to say I loved nothing so well as you, but believe
me not. And yet I lie not. I confess nothing, nor I deny nothing.
I am sorry for my cousin.

  BENEDICK   **By my sword, Beatrice, thou lovest me.**

  BEATRICE   **Do not swear, and eat it.**

380   **BENEDICK**   **I will swear by it that you love me. And I will make**
him eat it that says I love not you.

  BEATRICE   **Will you not eat your word?**

  BENEDICK   **With no sauce that can be devised to it. I protest I**
love thee.

  BEATRICE   **Why, then, God forgive me!**

390   **BENEDICK**   **What offence, sweet Beatrice?**

BEATRICE   **You have stayed me in a happy hour. I was about to protest I loved you.**

BENEDICK   **And do it with all thy heart.**

BEATRICE   **I love you with so much of my heart that none is left to protest.**

400   **BENEDICK**   **Come, bid me do any thing for thee.**

BEATRICE   **Kill Claudio.**

BENEDICK   **Ha! Not for the wide world.**

BEATRICE   **You kill me to deny it. Farewell.**

BENEDICK   **Tarry, sweet Beatrice.**

410   **BEATRICE**   **I am gone, though I am here. There is no love in you. – Nay, I pray you, let me go.**

BENEDICK   **Beatrice –**

BEATRICE   **In faith, I will go.**

BENEDICK   **We'll be friends first.**

BEATRICE   **You dare easier be friends with me than fight with**
420   **mine enemy.**

BENEDICK   **Is Claudio thine enemy?**

BEATRICE   **Is he not approved in the height a villain, that hath slandered, scorned, dishonoured my kinswoman? O that I were a man!** [What, bear her in hand until they come to take hands; and then, with public accusation, uncovered slander, unmitigated rancour -- O God, that I were a man!] **I would eat his heart in the market-place.**

430   [BENEDICK   Hear me, Beatrice --

BEATRICE   Talk with a man out at a window! A proper saying!]

BENEDICK   **Nay, but, Beatrice –**

BEATRICE   **Sweet Hero! She is wronged, she is slandered, she is undone.**

BENEDICK   **Beat–**
440

BEATRICE   [Princes and Counties! Surely, a princely testimony, a goodly count, Count Comfect; a sweet gallant, surely!] **O that I were a man for his sake! Or that I had any friend would be a man for my sake! But manhood is melted into curtsies, valour into compliment, and men are only turned into tongue ...** [and trim ones too. He is now as valiant as Hercules that only tells a lie and swears it.] **I cannot be a man with wishing, therefore I will die a woman with grieving.**

BENEDICK   **Tarry, good Beatrice. By this hand, I love thee.**
450

BEATRICE   **Use it for my love some other way than swearing by it.**

BENEDICK   Think you in your soul the Count Claudio hath wronged Hero?

BEATRICE   Yea, as sure as I have a thought or a soul.

BENEDICK   Enough, I am engaged. I will challenge him. I will kiss your hand, and so I leave you. By this hand, Claudio shall render me a dear account. As you hear of me, so think of me. Go, comfort your cousin. I must say she is dead – and so, farewell.   *(Exeunt)*

460

Scene 2   *[A prison.]*
Enter [the Constables] DOGBERRY, VERGES and the SEXTON in gowns, and [the Watch, with] CONRADE and BORACHIO.

DOGBERRY   Is our whole dissembly appeared?

VERGES   O, a stool and a cushion for the Sexton.

SEXTON   Which be the malefactors?

10

DOGBERRY   Marry, that am I and my partner.

[VERGES   Nay, that's certain. We have the exhibition to examine.]

SEXTON   But which are the offenders that are to be examined? Let them come before Master Constable.

DOGBERRY   Yea, marry, let them come before me. What is your name, friend?

20

BORACHIO   Borachio.

DOGBERRY   Pray, write down Borachio. – Yours, sirrah?

CONRADE   I am a gentleman, sir, and my name is Conrade.

DOGBERRY   Write down, 'Master Gentleman Conrade.' [Masters, do you serve God?

30   BOTH   Yea, sir, we hope.]

DOGBERRY   [Write down, that they hope they serve God. And write 'God' first, for God defend but God should go before such villains!] **Masters, it is proved already that you are little better than false knaves.** [And it will go near to be thought so shortly.] **How answer you for yourselves?**

CONRADE   Marry, sir, we say we are none.

DOGBERRY   A marvellous witty fellow, I assure you, but I will go about with him. Come you hither, sirrah. A word in your ear. Sir, I say to you, it is thought you are false knaves.

40

BORACHIO   Sir, I say to you we are none.

DOGBERRY   Well, stand aside. 'Fore God, they are both in a tale. Have you writ down, that they are none?

SEXTON   Master Constable, you go not the way to examine. You must call forth the watch that are their accusers.

50 **DOGBERRY** Yea, marry, that's the eftest way. Let the watch come forth. Masters, I charge you, in the Prince's name, accuse these men.

1st WATCH. This man said, sir, that Don John, the Prince's brother, was a villain.

DOGBERRY Write down Prince John a villain. Why, this is flat perjury, to call a prince's brother villain.

60 **BORACHIO** Master Constable –

DOGBERRY Pray thee, fellow, peace. I do not like thy look, I promise thee.

SEXTON What heard you him say else?

2nd WATCH. Marry, that he had received a thousand ducats of Don John for accusing the Lady Hero wrongfully.

70 [DOGBERRY Flat burglary as ever was committed.

VERGES Yea, by mass, that it is.]

SEXTON What else, fellow?

1st WATCH. And that Count Claudio did mean, upon his words, to disgrace Hero before the whole assembly, and not marry her.

80 **DOGBERRY** O villain! Thou wilt be condemned into everlasting redemption for this.

SEXTON What else?

1st WATCH. This is all.

SEXTON And this is more, masters, than you can deny. Prince John is this morning secretly stolen away. Hero was in this manner accused, in this very manner refused, and upon the grief
90 of this suddenly died. Master Constable, let these men be bound, and brought to Leonato's. I will go before and show him their examination. *(Exit)*

DOGBERRY Come, let them be opinioned.

[VERGES Let them be in the hands --]

CONRADE Off, coxcomb!

100 **DOGBERRY** God's my life, where's the Sexton? Let him write down the Prince's officer coxcomb. Come, bind them. Thou naughty varlet!

CONRADE Away! You are an ass, you are an ass.

DOGBERRY Dost thou not suspect my place? Dost thou not suspect my years? O that he were here to write me down an ass! But, masters, remember that I am an ass. Though it be not written down, yet forget not that I am an ass. No, thou villain, thou art full
110 of piety, as shall be proved upon thee by good witness. I am a wise

113

fellow, and, which is more, an officer, and, which is more, a householder, and, which is more, as pretty a piece of flesh as any is in Messina, and one that knows the law, go to. [And a rich fellow enough, go to. And a fellow that hath had losses, and one that hath two gowns and every thing handsome about him.] **Bring him away. O that I had been writ down an ass!**

(Exeunt)

ACT FIVE
Scene 1   *[Outside Leonato's house.]*
                    Enter LEONATO and ANTONIO.

ANTONIO   If you go on thus, you will kill yourself. And 'tis not wisdom thus to second grief Against yourself.

LEONATO   I pray thee, cease thy counsel,
10   **Which falls into mine ears as profitless As water in a sieve. Give not me counsel, Nor let no comforter delight mine ear But such a one whose wrongs do suit with mine. Bring me a father that so loved his child, Whose joy of her is overwhelmed like mine, And bid him speak of patience.**
    [Measure his woe the length and breadth of mine
    And let it answer every strain for strain,
    As thus for thus and such a grief for such,
20   In every lineament, branch, shape, and form.
    If such a one will smile and stroke his beard,
    Bid sorrow wag, cry 'hem' when he should groan,
    Patch grief with proverbs, make misfortune drunk
    With candle-wasters -- bring him yet to me,
    And I of him will gather patience.
    But there is no such man; for, brother, men
    Can counsel and speak comfort to that grief
    Which they themselves not feel; but, tasting it,
    Their counsel turns to passion, which before
30   Would give preceptial medicine to rage,
    Fetter strong madness in a silken thread,
    Charm ache with air and agony with words.]
    No, no, 'tis all men's office to speak patience To those that wring under the load of sorrow, But no man's virtue nor sufficiency To be so moral when he shall endure The like himself. Therefore give me no counsel. My griefs cry louder than advertisement.

40   **ANTONIO   Therein do men from children nothing differ.**

LEONATO   I pray thee, peace. I will be flesh and blood; For there was never yet philosopher

That could endure the toothache patiently –
[However they have writ the style of gods
And made a push at chance and sufferance.]

ANTONIO   Yet bend not all the harm upon yourself.
Make those that do offend you suffer too.

50

LEONATO   There thou speak'st reason. Nay, I will do so.
**My soul doth tell me Hero is belied,
And that shall Claudio know. So shall the Prince
And all of them that thus dishonour her.**

ANTONIO   Here comes the Prince and Claudio hastily.

Enter DON PEDRO and CLAUDIO.

60   **D. PEDRO**   Good den, good den.

CLAUDIO   Good day to both of you.

LEONATO   Hear you, my lords –

D. PEDRO   We have some haste, Leonato ...

LEONATO   Some haste, my lord? Well, fare you well, my lord.
Are you so hasty now? Well, all is one.

70

D. PEDRO   Nay, do not quarrel with us, good old man.

ANTONIO   If he could right himself with quarrelling,
Some of us would lie low.

CLAUDIO   Who wrongs him?

LEONATO   Marry, thou dost wrong me, thou dissembler, thou!
– Nay, never lay thy hand upon thy sword.
80   [I fear thee not.]

CLAUDIO   [Marry, beshrew my hand,
If it should give your age such cause of fear.]
In faith, my hand meant nothing to my sword.

LEONATO   Tush, tush, man. Never fleer and jest at me.
I speak not like a dotard nor a fool,
[As under privilege of age to brag
What I have done being young, or what would do
90   Were I not old.] **Know, Claudio, to thy head,
Thou hast so wronged mine innocent child and me
That I am forced to lay my reverence by
And, with grey hairs and bruise of many days,
Do challenge thee to trial of a man.
I say thou hast belied mine innocent child.
Thy slander hath gone through and through her heart,
And she lies buried with her ancestors.**
[O, in a tomb where never scandal slept,
Save this of hers, framed by thy villainy!
100

CLAUDIO   My villainy?

LEONATO   Thine, Claudio. Thine, I say!]

115

D. PEDRO   You say not right, old man.

LEONATO   My lord, my lord,
I'll prove it on his body – if he dare.
[Despite his nice fence and his active practice,
110   His May of youth and bloom of lustihood.]

CLAUDIO   Away, I will not have to do with you.

LEONATO   Canst thou so daff me? Thou hast killed my child.
If thou kill'st me, boy, thou shalt kill a man.

ANTONIO   He shall kill two of us, and men indeed.
But that's no matter. Let him kill one first.
[Win me and wear me! Let him answer me!]
120   Come, follow me, boy. Come, sir boy, come, follow me!
[Sir boy, I'll whip you from your foining fence!
Nay, as I am a gentleman, I will.]

LEONATO   Brother –

ANTONIO   Content yourself. God knows I loved my niece ...
And she is dead, slandered to death by villains –
[That dare as well answer a man indeed
As I dare take a serpent by the tongue.
130   Boys, apes, braggarts, Jacks, milksops!]

LEONATO   Brother Antony –

ANTONIO   Hold you content. What, man, I know them! – Yea,
And what they weigh, even to the utmost scruple –
Scrambling, out-facing, fashion-monging boys
That lie and cog and flout, deprave and slander,
Go anticly, show outward hideousness,
And speak off half a dozen dangerous words,
140   How they might hurt their enemies, if they durst.
And this is all.

LEONATO   But, brother Antony –

ANTONIO   Come, 'tis no matter.
Do not you meddle. Let me deal in this.

D. PEDRO   Gentlemen both, we will not wake your patience.
My heart is sorry for your daughter's death.
150   But, on my honour, she was charged with nothing
But what was true and very full of proof.

LEONATO   My lord, my lord –

D. PEDRO   I will not hear you.

LEONATO   No? Come, brother, away! I will be heard.

ANTONIO   And shall, or some of us will smart for it.
160

            Exeunt LEONATO and ANTONIO.

D. PEDRO   See, see, here comes the man we went to seek.

Enter BENEDICK.

CLAUDIO   Now, signior, what news?

BENEDICK   Good day, my lord.

170

D. PEDRO   Welcome, signior. You are almost come to part almost a fray.

CLAUDIO   We had like to have had our two noses snapped off with two old men without teeth.

D. PEDRO   Leonato and his brother. What thinkest thou? Had we fought, I doubt we should have been too young for them.

180   BENEDICK   In a false quarrel there is no true valour. I came to seek you both.

CLAUDIO   We have been up and down to seek thee, for we are high-proof melancholy and would fain have it beaten away. Wilt thou use thy wit?

BENEDICK   It is in my scabbard. Shall I draw it?

[D. PEDRO   Dost thou wear thy wit by thy side?

190

CLAUDIO   Never any did so, though very many have been beside their wit. I will bid thee draw, as we do the minstrels: draw to pleasure us.]

D. PEDRO   As I am an honest man, he looks pale. – Art thou sick, or angry?

[CLAUDIO   What, courage, man! What though care killed a cat, thou hast mettle enough in thee to kill care.]

200   BENEDICK   Sir, [I shall meet your wit in the career, and you charge it against me.] I pray you choose another subject.

[CLAUDIO   Nay, then, give him another staff. This last was broke cross.]

D. PEDRO   By this light, he changes more and more. I think he be angry indeed.

[CLAUDIO   If he be, he knows how to turn his girdle.]

210   BENEDICK   Shall I speak a word in your ear?

CLAUDIO   God bless me from a challenge!

BENEDICK   *(Aside to CLAUDIO)* You are a villain. I jest not. I will make it good how you dare, with what you dare, and when you dare. Do me right, or I will protest your cowardice. You have killed a sweet lady, and her death shall fall heavy on you. Let me hear from you.

220   CLAUDIO   Well, I will meet you, so I may have good cheer.

[D. PEDRO   What, a feast, a feast?

CLAUDIO   I' faith, I thank him. He hath bid me to a calf's head and a capon -- the which if I do not carve most curiously, say my knife's naught. Shall I not find a woodcock too?]

BENEDICK   Sir, your wit ambles well. It goes easily.

230   **D. PEDRO**   I'll tell thee how Beatrice praised thy wit the other day. I said, thou hadst a fine wit. "True," said she, "a fine little one." "No," said I, "a great wit." "Right," says she, "a great, gross one." "Nay," said I, "a good wit." "Just," said she, "it hurts nobody." ["Nay," said I, "the gentleman is wise." "Certain," said she, "a wise gentleman." "Nay," said I, "he hath the tongues." "That I believe," said she, "for he swore a thing to me on Monday night, which he forswore on Tuesday morning -- there's a double tongue, there's two tongues." Thus did she, an hour together, trans-shape thy particular virtues.] **Yet at last she concluded with a sigh, thou wast the properest man in Italy.**

240

CLAUDIO   For the which she wept heartily and said she cared not.

D. PEDRO   Yea, that she did ... but yet, for all that, an if she did not hate him deadly, she would love him dearly. The old man's daughter told us all.

CLAUDIO   All, all! [And, moreover, God saw him when he was hid in the garden.]

250

D. PEDRO   But when shall we set the savage bull's horns on the sensible Benedick's head?

CLAUDIO   Yea, and text underneath, 'Here dwells Benedick, the married man'?

BENEDICK   Fare you well, boy. You know my mind. I will leave you now to your gossip-like humour. You break jests as braggarts do their blades, which God be thanked, hurt not. My lord, for your many courtesies I thank you. I must discontinue your company. Your brother the bastard is fled from Messina. You have among you killed a sweet and innocent lady. For my Lord Lackbeard there, he and I shall meet. And, till then, peace be with him. *(Exit)*

260

D. PEDRO   He is in earnest.

CLAUDIO   In most profound earnest. And, I'll warrant you, for the love of Beatrice.

270   **D. PEDRO**   And hath challenged thee?

CLAUDIO   Most sincerely.

D. PEDRO   What a pretty thing man is when he goes in his doublet and hose and leaves off his wit!

[CLAUDIO   He is then a giant to an ape, but then is an ape a doctor to such a man.]

D. PEDRO   But, soft you, let me be. [Pluck up, my heart, and be sad.] **Did**
280   **he not say, my brother was fled?**

Enter DOGBERRY, VERGES and the Watch, with CONRADE and BORACHIO.

DOGBERRY Come you, sir, if justice cannot tame you, she shall ne'er weigh more reasons in her balance. [Nay, an you be a cursing hypocrite once, you must be looked to.]

290 **D. PEDRO**   How now? Two of my brother's men bound, Borachio one?

CLAUDIO   Hearken after their offence, my lord.

D. PEDRO   Officers, what offence have these men done?

DOGBERRY Marry, sir, they have committed false report. Moreover, they have spoken untruths. Secondarily, they are slanders. Sixth and lastly, they have belied a lady. Thirdly, they have verified unjust things. And, to conclude, they are lying 300 knaves.

D. PEDRO   First, I ask thee what they have done. Thirdly, I ask thee what's their offence. Sixth and lastly, [why they are committed. And, to conclude,] what you lay to their charge.

CLAUDIO   Rightly reasoned, and in his own division. [And, by my troth, there's one meaning well suited.]

310 **D. PEDRO**   Who have you offended, masters, that you are thus bound to your answer? This learned constable is too cunning to be understood. [What's your offence?]

BORACHIO Sweet Prince, let me go no farther to mine answer. [Do you hear me, and let this count kill me. I have deceived even your very eyes.] What your wisdoms could not discover these shallow fools have brought to light -- who in the night overheard me confessing to this man how Don John your brother incensed me to slander the Lady Hero; how you were brought into the orchard and saw me court Margaret in Hero's garments -- how you disgraced her, when you 320 should marry her. [My villainy they have upon record, which I had rather seal with my death than repeat over to my shame.] The lady is dead upon mine and my master's false accusation, and, briefly, I desire nothing but the reward of a villain.

D. PEDRO   Runs not this speech like iron through your blood?

CLAUDIO   I have drunk poison whiles he uttered it.

330 **D. PEDRO**   But did my brother set thee on to this?

BORACHIO   Yea, and paid me richly for the practice of it.

D. PEDRO   He is composed and framed of treachery.
And fled he is upon this villainy.

CLAUDIO   Sweet Hero, now thy image doth appear
In the rare semblance that I loved it first.

DOGBERRY Come, bring away the plaintiffs. By this time our 340 sexton hath reformed Signior Leonato of the. And, masters, do not forget to specify, when time and place shall serve, that I am an ass.

VERGES   Here, here comes master Signior Leonato, and the
Sexton too.

Re-enter LEONATO and ANTONIO, with the SEXTON.

LEONATO   Which is the villain? Let me see his eyes,
That, when I note another man like him,
350   I may avoid him. Which of these is he?

BORACHIO   If you would know your wronger, look on me.

LEONATO   Art thou the slave that with thy breath hast killed
Mine innocent child?

BORACHIO   Yea, even I alone.

LEONATO   No, not so, villain. Thou beliest thyself.
360   Here stand a pair of honourable men —
A third is fled — that had a hand in it.
I thank you, Princes, for my daughter's death.
Record it with your high and worthy deeds.
'Twas bravely done, if you bethink you of it.

CLAUDIO   I know not how to pray your patience,
Yet I must speak. Choose your revenge yourself.
Impose me to what penance your invention
Can lay upon my sin. Yet sinned I not
370   But in mistaking.

D. PEDRO   By my soul, nor I.
[And yet, to satisfy this good old man,
I would bend under any heavy weight
That he'll enjoin me to.]

LEONATO   I cannot bid you bid my daughter live.
That were impossible. But, I pray you both,
Possess the people in Messina here
380   How innocent she died. [And if your love
Can labour ought in sad invention,
Hang her an epitaph upon her tomb
And sing it to her bones, sing it tonight.]
Tomorrow morning come you to my house,
And since you could not be my son-in-law,
Be yet my nephew. My brother hath a daughter,
Almost the copy of my child that's dead,
And she alone is heir to both of us.
Give her the right you should have given her cousin,
390   And so dies my revenge.

CLAUDIO   O noble sir,
Your over-kindness doth wring tears from me.
I do embrace your offer, and dispose
For henceforth of poor Claudio.

LEONATO   Tomorrow then I will expect your coming.
Tonight I take my leave. This naughty man
Shall face to face be brought to Margaret,

400 **Who I believe was packed in all this wrong,**
Hired to it by your brother.

BORACHIO   No, by my soul, she was not,
Nor knew not what she did when she spoke to me,
But always hath been just and virtuous
In any thing that I do know by her.

DOGBERRY Moreover, sir, which indeed is not under white and
black, this plaintiff here, the offender, did call me ass. I beseech
410 **you, let it be remembered in his punishment.** [And also, the watch heard
them talk of one 'Deformed'. They say he wears a key in his ear and a lock hanging by it,
and borrows money in God's name, the which he hath used so long and never paid that
now men grow hard-hearted and will lend nothing for God's sake.] **Pray you,**
examine him upon that point.

LEONATO   I thank thee for thy care and honest pains.

DOGBERRY Your worship speaks like a most thankful and
reverend youth, and I praise God for you.
420
LEONATO   There's for thy pains.

DOGBERRY   God save the Foundation!

LEONATO   Go, I discharge thee of thy prisoner, and I thank thee.

DOGBERRY I leave an arrant knave with your worship, which I
beseech your worship to correct yourself, for the example of
others. [God keep your worship, I wish your worship well.] **God restore you to**
430 **health! I humbly give you leave to depart. And if a merry meeting**
may be wished, God prohibit it! – Come, neighbour.

Exeunt DOGBERRY and VERGES.

LEONATO   Until tomorrow morning, lords, farewell.

ANTONIO   Farewell, my lords. We look for you tomorrow.

D. PEDRO   We will not fail.
440
CLAUDIO   Tonight I'll mourn with Hero.

LEONATO   *(To the Watch)*
Bring you these fellows on. – We'll talk with Margaret,
How her acquaintance grew with this lewd fellow.   *(Exeunt)*

Scene 2   *[Leonato's garden.]*
Enter BENEDICK and MARGARET, meeting.

BENEDICK   Pray thee, sweet Mistress Margaret, deserve well at
my hands by helping me to the speech of Beatrice.

MARGARET Will you then write me a sonnet in praise of my
beauty?

10 **BENEDICK   In so high a style, Margaret, that no man living shall come over it.** [For, in most comely truth, thou deservest it.]

MARGARET   To have no man come over me!   Why, shall I always keep below stairs?

[BENEDICK   Thy wit is as quick as the greyhound's mouth -- it catches.

MARGARET   And yours as blunt as the fencer's foils, which hit but hurt not.]

20 **BENEDICK   A most manly wit, Margaret – it will not hurt a woman. And so, I pray thee, call Beatrice.** [I give thee the bucklers.

MARGARET   Give us the swords. We have bucklers of our own.

BENEDICK   If you use them, Margaret, you must put in the pikes with a vice – and … they are dangerous weapons for maids.]

MARGARET   Well, I will call Beatrice to you, who I think hath legs.
(Exit)

30 **BENEDICK   And therefore will come.**
(Sings)   **The god of love,**
That sits above,
And knows me, and knows me,
How pitiful I deserve …

I mean in singing. [But in loving, Leander the good swimmer, Troilus the first employer of panders, and a whole bookful of these quondam carpet-mongers whose names yet run smoothly in the even road of a blank verse, why, they were never so truly 40 turned over and over as my poor self in love. Marry, I cannot show it in rhyme. I have tried. I can find out no rhyme to 'lady' but 'baby' – an innocent rhyme; for 'scorn' 'horn' – a hard rhyme; for 'school' 'fool' – a babbling rhyme. Very ominous endings.] **No, I was not born under a rhyming planet…** [nor I cannot woo in festival terms.] *(Enter BEATRICE)*   **Sweet Beatrice, wouldst thou come when I called thee?**

BEATRICE   Yea, signior, and depart when you bid me.

BENEDICK   O, stay but till then!
50

BEATRICE   'Then' is spoken. Fare you well now. And yet, ere I go, let me go with that I came … which is, with knowing what hath passed between you and Claudio.

BENEDICK   Only foul words – and thereupon I will kiss thee.

BEATRICE   Foul words is but foul wind, and foul wind is but foul breath[, and foul breath is noisome]; **therefore I will depart unkissed.**

60 **BENEDICK   Thou hast frighted the word out of his right sense, so forcible is thy wit. But I must tell thee plainly, Claudio undergoes my challenge; and either I must shortly hear from him, or I will subscribe him a coward. And, I pray thee now, tell me for which of my bad parts didst thou first fall in love with me?**

BEATRICE   For them all together, which maintained so politic a state of evil that they will not admit any good part to intermingle

with them. **But for which of my good parts did you first suffer love for me?**

70

BENEDICK 'Suffer' love! A good epithet! I do suffer love indeed, for I love thee against my will.

BEATRICE In spite of your heart, I think. Alas, poor heart! If you spite it for my sake, I will spite it for yours -- for I will never love that which my friend hates.

BENEDICK Thou and I are too wise to woo peaceably.

80 **BEATRICE** It appears not in this confession. There's not one wise man among twenty that will praise himself.

BENEDICK An old, an old instance, Beatrice, that lived in the time of good neighbours. If a man do not erect in this age his own tomb ere he dies, he shall live no longer in monument than the bell rings and the widow weeps.

[BEATRICE And how long is that, think you?

90 BENEDICK Question: why, an hour in clamour and a quarter in rheum.] **Therefore is it most expedient for the wise**[, if Don Worm – his conscience – find no impediment to the contrary,] **to be the trumpet of his own virtues, as I am to myself. So much for praising myself, who, I myself will bear witness, is praiseworthy. And now tell me, how doth your cousin?**

BEATRICE Very ill.

BENEDICK And how do you?

100

BEATRICE Very ill too.

BENEDICK Serve God, love me and mend. There will I leave you too, for here comes one in haste.

Enter URSULA.

URSULA Madam, you must come to your uncle. [Yonder's old coil at home.] **It is proved my Lady Hero hath been falsely accused, the Prince and Claudio mightily abused, and Don John is the author of all, who is fed and gone. Will you come presently?**

110

BEATRICE Will you go hear this news, signior?

BENEDICK I will live in thy heart, die in thy lap, and be buried in thy eyes -- and moreover I will go with thee to thy uncle's. *(Exeunt)*

Scene 3 *[A church.]*
Enter DON PEDRO and CLAUDIO [with three or four carrying tapers, and MUSICIANS].

CLAUDIO Is this the monument of Leonato?

LORD It is, my lord.

CLAUDIO   *(Reading from a scroll)*

10
'Done to death by slanderous tongues
Was the Hero that here lies.
Death, in guerdon of her wrongs,
Gives her fame which never dies.
So the life that died with shame
Lives in death with glorious fame.'   *(Hangs it up)*
'Hang thou there upon the tomb,
Praising her when I am dumb.'

20
[-- Now music sound, and sing your solemn hymn.

Song.
Pardon, goddess of the night,
Those that slew thy virgin knight;
For the which, with songs of woe,
Round about her tomb they go.
Midnight, assist our moan;
Help us to sigh and groan
    Heavily, heavily.
Graves, yawn and yield your dead,
30
Till death be utterèd,
    Heavily, heavily.]

CLAUDIO   **Now, unto thy bones good night.**
Yearly will I do this rite.

D. PEDRO   **Good morrow, masters. Put your torches out.**
The wolves have preyed, and – look – the gentle day,
Before the wheels of Phoebus, round about,
Dapples the drowsy east with spots of grey.
40
[Thanks to you all, and leave us. Fare you well.

CLAUDIO   Good morrow, masters. Each his several way.]

D. PEDRO   **Come, let us hence, and put on other weeds,**
And then to Leonato's we will go.

CLAUDIO   **And Hymen now with luckier issue speeds**
Than this for whom we rendered up this woe.   *(Exeunt)*

Scene 4   *[A room in Leonato's house.]*
Enter LEONATO, ANTONIO, BENEDICK, BEATRICE,
MARGARET, URSULA, FRIAR FRANCIS and HERO.

F. FRANCIS   **Did I not tell you she was innocent?**

LEONATO   **So are the Prince and Claudio, who accused her**
Upon the error that you heard debated.
[But Margaret was in some fault for this,
10
Although against her will, as it appears
In the true course of all the question.]

ANTONIO   **Well, I am glad that all things sort so well.**

BENEDICK   **And so am I, being else by faith enforced**

To call young Claudio to a reckoning for it.

LEONATO   Well, daughter, and you gentlewomen all,
Withdraw into a chamber by yourselves,
20   And when I send for you, come hither masked.   *(Exeunt Ladies)*
The Prince and Claudio promised by this hour
To visit me. You know your office, brother.
You must be father to your brother's daughter,
And give her to young Claudio.

ANTONIO   Which I will do with confirmed countenance.

BENEDICK   Friar, I must entreat your pains, I think.

30   **F. FRANCIS**   To do what, signior?

BENEDICK   To bind me or undo me – one of them.
Signior Leonato, truth it is, good signior,
Your niece regards me with an eye of favour.

LEONATO   That eye my daughter lent her, 'tis most true.

BENEDICK   And I do with an eye of love requite her.

40   **LEONATO**   The sight whereof I think you had from me,
From Claudio and the Prince. But what's your will?

BENEDICK   Your answer, sir, is enigmatical ...
But for my will, my will is: your good will
May stand with ours, this day to be conjoined
In the state of honourable marriage.
In which, good Friar, I shall desire your help.

LEONATO   My heart is with your liking.

50

F. FRANCIS   And my help.
– Here comes the Prince and Claudio.

    Enter DON PEDRO with CLAUDIO [and two or three others].

D. PEDRO   Good morrow to this fair assembly.

LEONATO   Good morrow, Prince, good morrow, Claudio.
We here attend you. Are you yet determined
60   Today to marry with my brother's daughter?

CLAUDIO   I'll hold my mind, were she an Ethiope.

LEONATO   Call her forth, brother. Here's the Friar ready.

    Exit ANTONIO.

D. PEDRO   Good morrow, Benedick. – Why, what's the matter,
That you have such a February face?
70   [So full of frost, of storm and cloudiness?]

CLAUDIO   I think he thinks upon the savage bull.
[Tush, fear not, man! We'll tip thy horns with gold
And all Europa shall rejoice at thee --
As once Europa did at lusty Jove,
When he would play the noble beast in love.]

BENEDICK   Bull Jove, sir, had an amiable low.
And some such strange bull leaped your father's cow
80   And got a calf in that same noble feat
Much like to you, for you have just his bleat.

Enter ANTONIO, with the LADIES masked.

CLAUDIO   For this I owe you. Here comes other reck'nings.
Which is the lady I must seize upon?

ANTONIO   This same is she, and I do give you her.

90   **CLAUDIO**   Why, then she's mine. – Sweet, let me see your face.

LEONATO   No, that you shall not, till you take her hand
Before this friar and swear to marry her.

CLAUDIO   Give me your hand ... Before this holy friar,
I am your husband, if you like of me.

HERO   And when I lived, I was your other wife – *(Unmasks)*
And when you loved, you were my other husband.
100
CLAUDIO   Another Hero!

HERO   Nothing certainer.
One Hero died defiled, but I do live,
And surely as I live, I am a maid.

D. PEDRO   The former Hero! Hero that is dead!

LEONATO   She died, my lord, but whiles her slander lived.
110
F. FRANCIS   All this amazement can I qualify.
When after that the holy rites are ended,
I'll tell you largely of fair Hero's death.
Meantime let wonder seem familiar,
And to the chapel let us presently.

BENEDICK   Soft and fair, Friar ... Which is Beatrice?

BEATRICE   *(Unmasks)* I answer to that name. What is your will?
120
BENEDICK   Do not you love me?

BEATRICE   Why, no. No more than reason.

BENEDICK   Why, then your uncle and the Prince and Claudio
Have been deceived. They swore you did.

BEATRICE   Do not you love me?

130   **BENEDICK**   Troth, no. No more than reason.

BEATRICE   Why, then my cousin Margaret and Ursula
Are much deceived. For they did swear you did.

BENEDICK   They swore that you were almost sick for me.

BEATRICE   They swore that you were well-nigh dead for me.

BENEDICK   'Tis no such matter. Then you do not love me?

140

BEATRICE   No, truly, but in friendly recompense.

LEONATO   Come, cousin, I am sure you love the gentleman.

CLAUDIO   And I'll be sworn upon it that he loves her,
For here's a paper written in his hand,
A halting sonnet of his own pure brain,
Fashioned to Beatrice.

150   **HERO**   And here's another,
Writ in my cousin's hand, stolen from her pocket,
Containing her affection unto Benedick.

BENEDICK   A miracle! Here's our own hands against our hearts.
Come, I will have thee. – But, by this light, I take thee for pity.

BEATRICE   I would not deny you – but, by this good day, I yield
upon great persuasion – and partly to save your life, for I was told
you were in a consumption.

160

BENEDICK   Peace! I will stop your mouth. *(Kisses her)*

D. PEDRO   How dost thou, Benedick, the married man?

BENEDICK   I'll tell thee what, Prince, a college of wit-crackers
cannot flout me out of my humour. Dost thou think I care for a
satire or an epigram? No. [If a man will be beaten with brains, 'a shall wear
nothing handsome about him.] In brief, since I do purpose to marry, I will
think nothing to any purpose that the world can say against it.
170   And therefore never flout at me for what I have said against it; for
man is a giddy thing, and this is my conclusion. For thy part,
Claudio, I did think to have beaten thee, but in that thou art like
to be my kinsman, live unbruised and love my cousin.

CLAUDIO   I had well hoped thou wouldst have denied Beatrice,
that I might have cudgelled thee out of thy single life to make thee
a double-dealer – which, out of question, thou wilt be, if my cousin
do not look exceedingly narrowly to thee.

180   **BENEDICK**   Come, come, we are friends. Let's have a dance ere
we are married, that we may lighten our own hearts and our
wives' heels.

LEONATO   We'll have dancing afterward ...

BENEDICK   First, of my word! Therefore play, music! Prince, thou
art sad – get thee a wife, get thee a wife! [There is no staff more reverend
than one tipped with horn.]

190   *Enter a MESSENGER.*

MESS.   My lord, your brother John is ta'en in flight,
And brought with armèd men back to Messina.

BENEDICK   Think not on him till tomorrow. I'll devise thee brave
punishments for him. – Strike up, pipers!

Dance. Exeunt.

OTHER BOOKS BY STEVE GOOCH
Writing a Play (A&C Black)
All Together Now (Methuen)

PLAYS BY STEVE GOOCH
Female Transport, about women convicts transported to Australia **(French)**
Will Wat, if not, what will? about Wat Tyler's Peasants' Revolt **(Pluto Press)**
The Motor Show (Pluto Press)
The Women Pirates Ann Bonney and Mary Read (Pluto Press)
Back Street Romeo (from Shakespeare)
Landmark (Theatre Action Press)
What They Want (from Terence's 'The Brothers')
McNaughton, monologue by the would-be assassin of a Prime Minister

BOYS AND GIRLS
Good for You *(1m, 1f)*, a 1980s office affair on the verge of splitting up
Star Turns *(2m,3f)*, suburban girlfriends seek the astrologically perfect man
Your Loving *(3m, 2f)*, Emma Goldman's unlikely affair with hobo Ben Reitman

MAINLY WOMEN
Massa *(2m, 7f)*, Victorian sociologist Arthur Munby's curious relationships with a
maid-of-all-work and the pit lasses of theWigan coalfields
British Beauty *(4m, 6f)*, how pre-Raphaelite Rossetti came to draw a simple
country girl at the Sussex home of women's rights campaigner, Barbara Bodichon
Cocky's Girls *(2m, 5f)*, the women in the working life of Alfred Hitchcock

AUTEURS
Dark Glory *(4m, 3f)*, the early, bohemian family life of Alfred Lord Tennyson
Free Time *(5m, 2f)*, 1930s poets in Barcelona during the Spanish Civil War
Asking Rembrandt *(3m, 1f)*, the painter interprets a commission his own way

MEANING BUSINESS
Bill of Health *(2m, 2f)*, health-conscious hippies turn a gym into a business
Handover *(3m, 2f)*, a high street print shop from grandfather to grandson
Running Wild *(6m, 2f)*, a couple's rural restoration project is foiled by nature

ADAPTATIONS BY STEVE GOOCH
Great Expectations
Man is Man
Candide
Ondine
Fuente Ovejuna
The Mother (Methuen)
St Joan of the Stockyards
Mister Paul
The Lulu Plays and The Marquis of Keith (Oberon Books)

Enquiries to The Narrow Road Company, 182 Brighton Road, Coulsdon, CR5 2NF